Kalyn's SECRET

Every Parent's Battle to Save Their Children

by Lisa and Kalyn Cherry

12 11 10 09   10 9 8 7 6 5 4 3 2 1

Kalyn's Secret: Every Parent's Battle to Save Their Children

ISBN: 978-0-88144-529-9
Copyright © 2009 by Lisa and Kalyn Cherry

Published by
Word and Spirit Resources
P.O. Box 701403
Tulsa, Oklahoma 74170
www.wordandspiritresources.com

Printed in Canada.

ENDORSEMENTS

While many families sweep issues under a rug, this family chose to sweep their daughter up in a life-changing tidal wave of mercy and grace instead! Through *Kalyn's Secret*, you'll be challenged and inspired to let God work through you in the lives of your children, no matter what kind of battles they face in life!

Shannon Ethridge, M.A.
Life Coach and Bestselling Author –
***Every Woman's Battle* series**

As a Dad and as a Husband – I want to do everything I can to protect my family. This book offers great insight to help prevent physical and spiritual attack from outside influences and is an incredible resource to help those already in the battle. It is a message of hope for all parents.

Michael W. Smith
Singer/Songwriter

Kalyn's Secret is a must read for every parent, pastor, youth minister and educator. It brings to light a very real issue that every society has to deal with in one way or another, and that is the issue of the predator. Whether they emerge in the form of a person, a drug, or a challenging disorder, the predator still comes to steal the hearts of children away from their families.

The Cherry's painful struggle and ultimate victory provides practical insight and wisdom to help you avoid the battle...and hope for those who find themselves in the midst of it. I highly recommend it.

Darlene Zschech
Singer/Songwriter

A must read for parents who want a glimpse of our declining culture's intrusion into a Christ-centered family and how God miraculously brought them through it.

Ron Luce
Director, Teen Mania Ministries/Acquire the Fire

Kalyn's Secret is a must-read for parents who are serious about their role in the lives of their children. This wonderful book is a godsend in our day and age of perversions and abuses of all kinds. Seen through the eyes of an abused and confused teenager as well as through the eyes of a mother (and family) not willing to give up on their child, *Kalyn's Secret* will bring to light vital truths to help any parent wage war against the enemy who desires to break down communication and bring destruction to every family. I strongly urge you to read this timely book.

Dennis Jernigan
Worship Leader/ Artist/Author/ Minister

I will never forget the night Doug Cherry tapped my husband's shoulder during a meeting and said, "We need your help. Please come with me." We follwed him to a secluded part of the building where we found Lisa, holding their newborn child, and their oldest daughter, Kalyn. We had never met Kalyn before, but it was obvious something was very wrong.

Lisa fell into my arms sobbing as she tried to explain what had happened. The report was difficult to comprehend. The circumstances were unbelievable and totally foreign to me. Kalyn was involved in a bad relationship, a "computer relationship", which had totally taken control of her life.

Light penetrated darkness that night as a battle began in the spirit to rescue Kalyn from a force she had totally embraced and was unwilling to walk away from. Lisa and Doug were amazing and unrelenting in their fight against the evil that held Kalyn deceived and imprisoned in her mind.

This book is a must read for parents today who have wrestled with nagging questions of 'what happened to my child' or 'where did my child go?' Though circumstances may differ, the solutions steps and tools contained in this book will enable them to gain the victory over their situation as well.

In Mark 9:23, Jesus said, 'If you can believe, all things are possible to him who believes.' This family believed, even in the toughest of times. They remained faithful to see and employ God's wisdom and today share the testimony of every family member walking in the fruit of this Scripture.

Pam Mickler, co-pastor
Victory Christian Center, Southbend, IN

As pastors, former youth pastors and parents of a daughter, we found Lisa and Kalyn's book to be both informative and timely. We are grateful that the Cherry's have been so transparent and honest about "Kayln's Secret" and the process they walked through as a family to receive healing and restoration. We highly recommend this book to any parent, youth worker or pastor. It will open your eyes to the all too prevalent problem of sexually abusive relationships and how to detect and deal with it in a Christ-like manner.

Hal & Lisa Boehm, Lead Pastors,
Summit Church, Elkins, WV
Directors of Catchfire! Ministries.

Parenting is not an easy task, but Doug and Lisa Cherry make it look simple. They are loving parents who are committed to raising their children to be close to God. Yet, in these modern times even the best families face dire attacks from the pits of hell. In this powerful book, Lisa explains how Satan attacked her daughter Kalyn. With heartfelt simplicity and profound insight, this book reveals how a family can emerge victorious from even the worst circumstances. The story of what the Cherry family went through will help you raise your family.

Daniel & Jessica King
Missionary Evangelists
King Ministries International

In *Kalyn's Secret* Kalyn and her mom rip the blinders off our eyes showing us a darkness we do not see and give concrete answers. Sharing their own guilt and confusion, they open their wounded souls until we actually feel their pain and weep with them as they share the dark night of a family's soul that lasted for years and yet by following "The Plan" God laid out for them they walked through in glorious victory.

This book should be mandatory reading in every School of Ministry everywhere. It should be required reading for every minister, minister's wife, teacher, youth leader, every preteen child, every church membership class, every premarital counseling, and certainly every parenting class should use it as a study guide.

I want all of my children and 16 grandchildren to read it. I wish with all my heart that I could have read it twenty-five years ago when a sexual predator/youth leader stole the childhood of two of my children...but like Lisa Cherry...I didn't know. But NOW we can know. Read *Kalyn's Secret.* It will change your life and save future generations for the Glory of God.

Wanda Winters-Guitierrez
Author of *The Search for Peace:*
A Woman's Guide to Spiritual Wholeness

Think this couldn't happen to you? Think again. I have referred to the crucial teachings in this book repeatedly throughout my own battle for our teenager's soul. This book will give you the confidence to resist the enemy with mountain-moving faith and a steadfast heart.

Lynne Davis
Parent of two teens –
Carbondale, IL

Lisa is a very gifted communicator and mentor. Those of us who have had the privilege of being a part of her Frontline Families Homeschool Mom's Group have greatly benefitted from her years of experience in raising godly children, her relational transparency and her practical, down-to-earth wisdom! This book is a must-read especially for strong Christian parents who desire to protect innocent daughters from the subtlety of the enemy's schemes and to equip us to live victoriously in these last days.

Jan Crall,
homeschool mom and senior pastor's wife
Calvary Campus Church, Carbondale, Illinois

One of my favorite authors said, 'God is always speaking and doing great things in the Kingdom. Find out what He is doing and join in.' God is speaking and doing great things through the ministry of Frontline Families. The book, *Kalyn's Secret* is the evidence. Join In.

Deanna Cohen
Mother of five –
REALITY Youth Center, Carbondale, IL

ACKNOWLEDGEMENTS

Kalyn's Secret never would have progressed past a stack of handwritten notes without the efforts of many caring, loving saints of God who caught hold of the book's vision to bring protection, hope and healing to a wounded generation.

To Jacqui, Lynne, Tara, Lisa, Lucas, Nathan and Pam who endured the countless writes and rewrites of two novice writers, we say thanks.

To Chaz, who believed in this book's potential from its inception.

To Karen, who adopted our project as her own and patiently positioned us for success. Thanks for the countless hours of extra work.

To our church family at Victory Christian Center who prayed, stood, and believed with us for a miracle.

To the Frontline Moms group, who willingly became guinea pigs for our first *Kalyn's Secret* study group.

To all our precious family: The Renshaw's, Groh's, Cherry's, Davis', and Mohr's, thanks for loving us in every season, every time.

To Adam, for your understanding, support and strength.

To Nathan, Tara, Lilibeth, Lucas, Rebekah, Hannah, Micah, Matthew, Ethan, Lydia and Josiah, you make our home and our lives overflow with laughter and joy. Each one of you make us proud!

To Doug, Lisa's best friend, confidante and knight in shining armor and Kalyn's daddy, carrier and friend, thanks for inspiring us and encouraging us every step of the way.

And most of all, to our Lord and Savior, Deliverer and Friend, Jesus...

Thanks for healing our hearts to sing again.

Lisa and Kalyn

Psalm 40

FOREWORD

When I read *Kalyn's Secret,* I could hardly put this book down. Not only was it shocking to the core to hear about such a beautiful family undergoing such a horrific nightmare, but I really believe this book has a message for every parent in this hour.

This generation coming up has been shaped by so many outside influences beyond family—internet, media, culture, etc. and so we parents face challenges that no other generation of parents have ever faced. Lisa so accurately diagnoses the parent/child conflicts and gives insightful, godly and practical help to overcome. She has done the research for us and very clearly and strategically maps out a rescue plan to take back our kids! Her background of post-modern and liberal thought gives her unique perspective on worldview that we MUST have in order to raise godly children in today's culture, because the world in which they are growing up in is on a fast track to post-modern thought.

Whether you are at your wit's end in your parenting and facing your own "dark night of the soul", or you are just going through the normal but sometimes excruciating frustrations of rebellion with your teenagers, I urge you to open the pages of this book and begin to learn how to get your family back to where God is on the throne!

Our children and teenagers are the future leaders of the church, this nation, and the world, and so it is critical that we as parents do what is necessary and mandated by God for this day and age to see their generation fulfill their destiny.

Katie Luce
Teen Mania Ministries

CONTENTS

INTRODUCTION:

Powering Up for the Journey

When my two oldest children, Nathan and Kalyn, were preschoolers, I (Lisa) remember believing what I had always heard. I thought my most intense years of mothering were nearing an end and a new, less demanding era was dawning. After all, diaper messes, milk spills, and toddler fusses require countless hours of hard work and effort. Surely as those babies grew into childhood and then into adolescence, they would be able to manage quite well without as much mothering input. That would leave me adequate time to pursue my own career and personal interests. Makes sense.

Why is it that no one warned me about the absurdity of my notions? Or did they, and I just didn't believe it? I guess when I formed my plans I hadn't calculated in the massive, intense warfare that is being waged against this teenage generation and their future. I underestimated the strategic cunning of the spiritual forces of darkness to develop fortresses in our homes. Oh, my husband, Doug, and I were aware of the battle. We had taken what we thought were radical measures to insure our escape from its effects. We had sheltered our children from the cultural onslaught and trained them to stand for God. We, as a family, were close, strong, and passionate in service to our King. So what happened to my daughter Kalyn should not have happened—but it did.

When Kalyn was 15 years old, we discovered that she had been subtly drawn into a sexually abusive relationship with one of our male parishioners who was three decades older than her, and it had been going on for over a year. Suddenly our world was turned upside down as the enemy launched his masterful sneak attack against our family in our own living room the day we learned of Kalyn's "secret." Our lives were shaken to the core and as a family we would never be the same again. That day rocked our very souls as we watched our high-achieving, mature, Christian daughter instantly transformed into a depressed, angry, defiant, rebellious, (and soon after) self-mutilating, suicidal teenager.

I was not prepared in the natural for what had come against Kalyn or the aftermath of the intense battle that raged against our family. Yet I am so grateful to all who had discipled and prepared us to face our opponent in the power of Jesus Christ. So many parents are under-prepared (spiritually and naturally) for their day of attack, whether it comes by sexual abuse, drugs, or other surprise tactics the enemy uses against unsuspecting, unaware families. Kalyn and I hope to change that through our story.

What special insights can an ordinary Midwestern pastor's family offer to other families at war? Mostly this—we have been to the foxhole *and have come back victorious*. What we knew before our attack was vital to our daughter's miracle. What we learned during and after our attack has compelled us to write this book to serve two main purposes: to be a signal flare to warn other families, and a boot camp training manual to help them understand the times and know how to safely navigate what can quickly become turbulent waters during the Journey through adolescence.

We'll be revealing important practical and scriptural keys to rescuing or keeping this generation from disaster, while candidly telling of our own intense personal crisis. By openly sharing our weaknesses as well as our strengths, our failures as well as our victories, we want to expose the deeds of darkness while we awaken and equip you as a parent (or grandparent or legal guardian) to aggressively defend your home from darkness and offensively advance God's plans for your family.

At no other season of my children's lives have I been called on to live in such unlikely extremes of balance—relevant, yet not trendy; playful, yet not childish; wise, yet not antiquated; and flexible, yet not indecisive—as during the Journey through adolescence. Good thing I had a few years to grow up myself before I stepped into this job. I figure with another decade of experience, I might have the required balancing act mastered! I suppose that's why the adolescent parenting sections of bookstores are overflowing with manuals to assist the flustered parent.

This season of parenthood is so challenging because adolescents themselves are so challenged. Some days their lives make no sense, even to them: one moment they're mature and level-headed; the next it seems as if they've reverted back to a toddler in their decision-making. Moreover, the average teen doesn't enjoy living like most of the rest of the world. They are looking for that "new" or "cool" place where they can "do it my way." Thus, we stand by as our own child changes before our very eyes.

While the outward physical changes are obvious and pronounced, the inward changes are perhaps even more spectacular and mysterious. So, here's the radical new conclusion that I've drawn about the parenting career: Don't expect to power down as you round into this Journey through adolescence. Be prepared to power *up*! And fasten your seat belt. You're in for an adventurous ride!

I pray that, like us, once you grab hold of the truths in this book, never again will you underestimate the strength of our opponent or pridefully believe that you've "done it all" to protect your children. And never again will you doubt the miracle-working power of our Captain (Heb. 2:10) and King to bring beauty for ashes, joy for mourning, and victory for defeat.

Your life is a journey you must travel
with a deep consciousness of God
—1 PETER 1:18 MSG

CHAPTER 1

Everything's Under
Control...Or Is It?

B *eep, beep, beep, my alarm screamed as I hit the off*
button before it could wake anyone else. Two A.M.
Lying motionless on the bed, I strained to hear any
sound of movement within the house. All was quiet. Breathing
a sigh of relief, I swung my legs out from under the comforter
as my warm, sleepy body braced itself for the cold. The
moment my feet hit the floor I quickly and quietly slipped on
my shoes and sweatshirt and tiptoed into the hallway.
Squinting in the darkness, I made a quick scan of the rooms.
Reassured that all of my siblings were still asleep, I padded
silently toward Mom's and Dad's bedroom. Pressing my ear to
the door, I listened for movement. Whew, no sound. So far, so
good. Feeling my way through the darkened house, I inched
my way to the basement, where my older brother slept.
Pausing to ensure the depth of his sleep, I slipped silently
through the room and out the creaky door.

Seconds later the cool air washed over me as I stepped outside and crept to the front of the house where Dad's black Grand Marquis was parked in the drive. Why was it always parked right outside my parents' bedroom window? I grabbed the door handle of the driver's side and pulled. The loud click of the door seemed to echo in the night. My pounding heart pulsated in my ears as I waited again for sign of movement. When I felt it was safe to proceed, I climbed into the sedan in search of the small electronic device that seemed to control me. Success! My fingers curled around the cold hard case of Dad's cell phone. Protectively, I drew it close and began my retreat from the car, holding my breath once again as I made sure the car door had clicked completely closed. Why do car doors have to slam to turn the light off?

The moonlight lit a clear path as I walked to the detached garage, holding the prized possession in hand. Reaching into my pocket, I pulled out the small slip of paper. Smoothing out the wrinkles, I scanned the numerous numbers that had been scribbled down over the last few weeks. Calling-card numbers, hotel numbers from different states, and pin numbers. What a mess! With fingers shaking, I carefully selecting the digits I needed that night.

Although only a few seconds passed, the wait seemed like an eternity. Would he answer? My heart raced as I heard the familiar voice on the other line—the voice that simultaneously brought me comfort and torment. A wave of both fear and excitement rushed through my body. Surely no one would ever know. ...

O full of all deceit and all fraud,...you enemy of all righteousness, will you not cease perverting the straight ways [or journey[1]] of the Lord?

ACTS 13:10 NKJV

An Allegory of the Journey Through Adolescence

Once upon a time in the faraway land of Reality ran the beautiful winding Maturity River. All the inhabitants of Reality were familiar with this waterway, for most of them had journeyed or would eventually journey on the Maturity at least twice during their lives. Their first required journey early in life left some with memories that were sweet and pleasant; for others, they were frightening and harsh. Their subsequent journeys on the river would prove defining in the lives of their own children.

Every resident who began the journey down the river received the same standard issue boat for the ride—a two-seater with a low horsepower inboard motor. The boat's controls were on the starboard side, and in the stern was a small cargo hold with a special trap door to store important needed gear for the journey. Though it had a small motor, the boat only traversed the river one direction— downstream from the head to the mouth.

On a fine sunny day in August of a recent year, the boat launch was ablaze with activity as new passengers were preparing to embark on their long anticipated journey. One such family enthusiastically approached the boat launch and as they were issued their boat, Child clapped her hands in glee as Parent listened for instruction. Parent was on the starboard side of the boat manning the controls and Child assumed the passenger side. As their journey began, Parent confidently navigated the boat down the slow, winding river. Both Parent and Child enjoyed their leisurely journey. Every now and then Child jumped over on Parent's lap to help steer, but Parent never took his hands off the wheel and Child dutifully assumed her regular seat when she was done "play driving."

After a long season of pleasant cruising, suddenly the family's boat encountered a river blockade. All boats were commanded to pull over to the riverside so that adjustments to the boats could be made. The family dutifully exited theirs and approached the shore officer as he was making an important announcement. "All boat captains will soon return to your boats and proceed on your journey, but with new boating arrangements. Parents, you will now sit in the passenger seat. Child, you have now come of age to assume the starboard side. However, Parent, remember that though the child is now driving, *you* are still the boat's captain and ultimately in charge.

"Each Child is being given a new name—Teen. Listen well to your boat captain. Receive their instruction. Listen for their counsel as you learn to steer your boat. And watch carefully ahead, for you are headed into dangerous territory. The waters move swiftly, the shoreline is rocky and jagged, and hidden throughout your passageway are camouflaged boulders that are sharp, protruding, and dangerous. Proceed cautiously lest your boat run aground on one of them. And remember, many have found the river current especially strong, luring, and dangerous.

When the family returned to their boat, parent was shocked by his new seating arrangement. He felt the day had come prematurely. Child—now Teen—was thrilled. It was the day she had been waiting for! She had finally made it to the driver's seat.

A New Kind of Maneuvering

Their boat was launched back on the river to continue its journey. As it began to sway back and forth, Teen adjusted her wheel to experiment with her master controls. Parent had never experienced this kind of maneuvering before. "Stop! Turn left! Watch out!" he shouted. Would the boat stay on course with Teen at the wheel? Parent wasn't at all sure it could, so he jumped out of his seat and began frantically rummaging around the cargo hold for the instruction manual placed there by the boat manufacturer. If he wasn't able to take back the controls of the boat himself, surely he could find some extra help in that manual to train and instruct Teen in boat driving! Oh, how Parent wished he had studied the manual during those years of peaceful sailing—before Child became Teen.

While the boat occupants were distracted—Parent with searching the hull and Teen by playing with the controls—"It" came into sight. "It" was tall and booming, yet strangely attractive, and was just as it had been described. Daunting. Looming. Jagged. Magnificent. An island boulder named Alcohol, "it" was a mysteriously welcoming inlet, perfectly sized for the little boat to enter and easy to access because of the drawing force of the current. Teen seemed enamored with the island boulder's presence. As she steered their little boat for a closer look, Parent realized they were mere seconds away from running ashore. "Stop! Danger! Turn starboard, *now!*"

Teen, shocked by Parent's boisterous outburst, jerked the steering wheel right and at just the last possible moment missed the shores of Alcohol.

"Whew, that was a close call," muttered Parent as he sank back in his seat. "Thank God, we didn't run aground." He sighed as his head sank to his hands.

"Oh Parent, I had everything under control," retorted Teen. "We weren't going to crash! Besides, that stupid shore officer probably hasn't even been to Alcohol himself. He's just read some dismal book about it. It looked perfectly fine to me. I could've landed us safely in the inlet between those rocky edges. I'm sure of it. We wouldn't have been hurt, Parent. Just don't worry about it. Everything's fine."

Parent was shocked by Teen's response to their narrow escape from danger. Was this reaction by Teen due to ignorance, naivety, inexperience, rebellion or pride? Parent concluded it was a challenging mixture of all five. Whatever the source, the resulting foolishness was alarming. Parent vowed to keep a closer eye on the horizon and spend some extra time in the operation training manual he had found in the boat's compartment. Maybe he could learn something about those islands still ahead.

Smooth Sailing (or So It Seems)

Days, weeks, then months went by. Teen had now become accustomed to her role as driver, but Parent still struggled to embrace his role as captain. Parent had studied the names of the other "islands" their boat needed to avoid—*Depression, Drugs, Sexual Abuse, Rebellion, Violence, Teen Pregnancy*—and he certainly didn't intend to get their boat caught up on any of them! As day by day they encountered one of those islands, Teen seemed smugly indifferent to their presence, but Parent was mindful of each island's dangerously alluring currents. Still, after successfully passing several of them, even Parent was feeling more confident of their journey's success without mishap.

His strategy thus far was simple and seemed effective: he would inform Teen of the island names, command Teen to steer clear of them, and then watch Teen maneuver the boat away from danger. So far they had steered clear of the islands of Alcohol, Teen Pregnancy, Smoking, and Drug Abuse so Parent was gaining confidence in his plan. The next island—Sexual Abuse—Parent was sure wouldn't be a problem for Teen. Parent had already taken care of that one years ago when Teen was Child. He had taught her well so he was confident that Teen wouldn't even get close to being entrapped by that boulder.

Unfortunately, Parent had never done any research about the inhabitants of Sexual Abuse Island. Otherwise, he would have known those inhabitants didn't behave like the inhabitants of some of the more familiar islands. The sinister inhabitants of Sexual Abuse don't wait for the boat to land on their island. They have an amazing ability to jump onto a boat as it sails nearby and land on their victims' boats unseen and undetected. After entering a boat, the sneaky inhabitants of Sexual Abuse like to hide in the cargo hold of the unsuspecting vessels, waiting until a later time to make their presence known.

When the island of Sexual Abuse came into sight, the family performed its usual maneuvers. Teen sailed the boat up near to the boulders, and Parent's command immediately pulled her away from the shore. But, as they sailed past that island and their backs were now facing its shores, silently, stealthily a fiendish inhabitant of Sexual Abuse landed on their deck, opened the cargo hatch, and slipped into the hull beneath the ship. Parent and Teen were oblivious to his presence, and, unbeknownst to them, his strange dark powers were now at work on their boat.

Parent and Teen joked and teased with each other as the days of their journey continued. Every now and then they would wave at the other boats riding past them on the river Maturity. Some of those boat passengers were relaxed and jovial in spirit and would also shout back words of greeting. Parent was learning to relax in his role and even enjoy it at times—except whenever a fellow passing boat would sail by in what appeared to be a state of confusion and despair. They would watch in horror as some of those boats ran aground on the rocky islands. Those scenes were never pretty. Their troubling sight would disrupt the confident composure of both Parent and Teen, but never for long.

They were a successful team, and they were confident they could complete their journey without mishap—until that horrible day that neither Parent nor Teen ever thought would happen. The day when the dark powers of their unseen guest came to light and he exerted his own control over where their boat would sail. The day that all the torturous darkness of Sexual Abuse overpowered their young boat driver and forced her on the collision course with the twin islands of Rebellion and Depression. The day when the innocence of their boat journey was shattered by their own great quest of survival...

October 19, 2002, began as most any other day in our larger-than-average household of eleven—laundry, dishes, diapers, toys, music, laughter, and an occasional squabble. With nine children (at that time) ranging in age from 18 years to six weeks, no day concluded without its share of hills and valleys. For me (Lisa), the mother of such a large brood, this day was, like most, a delightful smorgasbord of mothering opportunities. Basketball practicing, potty training, college planning, newborn nursings, and fraction reducing would be expected of me, and I loved every part of it.

"I don't see how you do it!" is the comment I often hear in the grocery line. "I don't know how I do it either," I usually reply, "if it weren't for the power of God." This is especially true when you also factor in the other part of our family's unusual lifestyle. My husband, Doug, and I work together to pastor a growing, young church. Our lives are busy, challenging, exciting, and fun. I always did consider myself as coming from hardy stock. It's like living life in the extreme, and I wouldn't want it any other way.

With his usual humor, high energy, and joy, Doug led this crew with optimism, patience, and rock-solid faith. In fact, the whole Cherry tribe was known around town as that pastor's family in the white 15-passenger van with lots of kids who all get along amazingly well and seem to love each other dearly. Close, connected, devoted, hard-working, honest, talented, clean-cut, and fun—that was the community picture. All the more reason October 19 was such a shock.

Oh, to have the opportunity to live that day over again. Not that it was fun or good or satisfying or pretty, but what I wouldn't give to be able to relive that Saturday through the eyes of my present understanding. That's how life is sometimes; we are thrust out onto the center stage of a real-life drama and must make decisions on things we know very little about. It can be really humbling and humiliating, even looking back today.

Shattered Innocence

That Saturday was a busy day filled with last-minute lists and suitcases. Half of the Cherry family was preparing to depart for our church's annual leadership conference in Tulsa, Oklahoma. The other half of the clan was preparing to depart for a stay with grandmas and granddads. Having lived in Tulsa for five years, visiting there was always a welcome haven of sweet friendships and spiritual renewal. Little did we know that one of those last-minute trip preparations was about to uncover the horrible secret that would soon turn our world upside down.

Doug had sat down to pay a stack of bills before our departure, when he came across a monthly cell phone bill for over $800—one-and two-hour phone calls all made to another cell phone number and all in the middle of the night. He didn't know why it was on our bill and vowed he wasn't going to bed without answers. So a late-night family investigation was launched. The phone number was quickly identified. Perhaps, we reasoned, this was a billing error or a computer malfunction. But as each family member was individually questioned, no plausible explanation emerged except one. Interrogation soon led to confrontation with horrifying results—a secret relationship existed between a 46-year-old man from our congregation and our 15-year-old daughter, Kalyn. Surely this must be some kind of sick joke!

Shock. Accusation. Denial. Anger. Crying. Kalyn, Doug, and I became locked in a middle-of-the-night sea of emotions that none of us was equipped to understand.

Wasn't this just some sort of odd schoolgirl crush? If so, then why was the emotional response from our daughter so intense, so desperate, so bizarre? Why was she making ridiculous claims that this relationship was now "her whole life," and she couldn't possibly live without this man? How could *she claim that this man would be her future husband? Why was she pushing us away claiming we just wouldn't ever understand? Understand what? It soon became apparent that innocence—both hers and ours—had been shattered. Family trust had been violated and in a split second of time, the precious young daughter we thought we knew seemed to disappear. As a thick cloud of darkness enveloped our home, the minutes stretched into hours with confusion and despair gripping our souls.*

Perhaps it's really not so bad, *my optimistic mind tried to claim. Maybe we could just pray, go to bed, and then discover with the morning light that the ominous dark cloud had cleared. Perhaps Sunday morning will just progress as normal with order and peace.*

That shocking night we didn't understand that the strange relationship between our daughter and this man was really a case of criminal abuse. After all, abuse is something that just happens to "non-supervising" families; and real abuse always involves major physical access and contact between perpetrator and victim—right?

We didn't understand the effects of this abuse: the deep, intricate soul wounds inflicted on an adolescent and the shame and self-condemnation that were so carefully concealed in Kalyn behind a confident, bubbly, high-achieving teen exterior; the twisted reasoning and sophisticated denial systems that kept a young mind insulated from ugly truths and memories she had no way of handling; the intense emotional energy it required for a normally honest child to participate in a cover-up that had remained undiscovered for almost two years. Kalyn's mind had been carefully programmed by the perpetrator to believe that she was now the "black sheep" of the family. Her soul was locked in a battle with sexual perversity, and her life was compartmentalized into multiple lifestyles.

Doug and I hadn't a clue that we ourselves had fallen prey to the parental version of an incredibly powerful, effective, deceptive, and subtle grooming process that had allowed a sexually perverse man near our daughter. Our own overpowering emotional weights of shame, anger, embarrassment, and confusion taunted us with the hideous question of, "How could we possibly have not seen what was happening?"

On that horrifying night, our own parental soul wounds blinded our eyes from discernment and compassion. We didn't recognize our whole family was under the influence of what experts called "post abuse trauma." Little did we know that it would take us over a year to fully uncover all of what had happened to Kalyn and then another 5-plus years for the courts to finish dealing with our criminal case. Nor did we recognize the powerful spiritual forces of darkness that had developed fortresses in our own home.

Sunday morning dawned after nearly no sleep. When the alarm rang, I remember asking Doug if perhaps I had just experienced some kind of bad dream. I've jokingly asked that kind of silly question before, but this was different. I was absolutely serious. My shocked and traumatized mind refused to believe that something this ugly could have possibly happened in our home. Model families simply don't have this kind of problem!

We thought of canceling going to church and also our trip to Tulsa but decided not to—we never had been quitters, and life had to go on. Other people were depending on us, and Kalyn, for some reason, still wanted to go. Perhaps the trip to Tulsa might just snap some sense into the confusing situation.

Our peaceful vacation escape did not materialize. Instead, the horrible situation intensified like a snowball rolling downhill picking up more strength as it goes. Who was this child now living in our midst? Her physical features looked different. Her face was hard, drawn, and pale. With the usual twinkle gone, her eyes were sad, cold, and lifeless. Our normally levelheaded, intelligent daughter was now angry, rebellious, defiant, and withdrawn; even after hours of discussion, she remained stubbornly convinced that her parents were crazy to have a problem with this unlawful secret relationship.

Desperate for a Miracle

To recall the memories of those next weeks and months is like looking back on the scenes of a bad movie. Moments of horror stand out. Like the day I called the family counselor at Focus on the Family Ministries. After listening to the story of what we knew at that point had happened to Kalyn, the counselor kindly explained that though there did not appear to have been physical sexual contact in this relationship, the psychological damage caused by the Internet and phone exploitation could be very severe. We would need expert help to pull her out of the depression, rebellion, and premature emotional separation from her family that would likely result—and the recovery could take years.

Or like the days when I couldn't get Kalyn to pull her head out from under her bed covers, or drink water, or take food. I helplessly watched her grow thinner and thinner. I tried all the parenting tricks I could think of, but how do you threaten to take a privilege away from someone who claims she wants to die?

Or like the hours of great pain and torture when Kalyn would wander away from the house, and we had to search for evidence as to whether she intended to hurt herself, run away, or come back safely.

Or like the memories of my forced smiles designed to hide the awful realities of our family's problems from my very frightened young children who were trying to understand what was wrong with their big sister.

Or like the day we found it strangely comforting to finally have a medical expert tell us that adolescent clinical depression following her trauma could be contributing to Kalyn's angry, defiant behavior and irrational thought processes. Put our child on anti-depressant medication? For parents who didn't even use Tylenol very quickly, we were strangely eager to try anything that could help save our little girl.

With each passing day, then week, then month, we grew more desperate for answers, for emotional and physical strength, for peace, for hope, for help—for a miracle.

CHAPTER 2

Trapped, Torn, Addicted, and Confused

Kalyn wrote this chapter in 2005 when she was only 18 years old. Even though I had lived the nightmare with her, I was shocked when I first read her raw explanation of the pain she endured. We have preserved her original writing to provide a glimpse into the secret teenage world.

As a member of a pastor's family, I [Kalyn] found security in our tight-knit clan. Our brood was larger than average in love as well as in size, and for as long as I could remember, family was always the priority. From fun nights at home to summer vacations, we enjoyed being together and loved one another dearly. We had been through our share of troubling times and good times, but in the end, our family always stood strong.

Early in my life, I gave my heart to Jesus, surrendering my future to Him. Having been raised in the ways of the Lord, I learned to live my life with purpose every day. As I grew, I encouraged others in their faith and was alarmed when someone I knew fell away from God. Never willing to be moved in my beliefs, I plowed through life with a passion and joy that was evident to all those around me.

I held many roles in both the family life and in our newly growing church. As an active participator in drama, music, and children's ministries, I performed my duties well and left none to question my devotion. My sophomore year in the Cherry home school was coming along just fine. When left to manage the household, I gave it my all, changing diapers and feeding tots like a pro.

I seemed to be maturing rapidly in all areas of my life. Never afraid to take on more responsibility, I functioned in leadership positions surprisingly well for a fifteen-year-old girl. I was a well-respected, mature, godly, dependable girl and appeared to be confidently on my way to an incredible future full of joy and success. No one could have guessed the pain, turmoil, and bondage that filled my soul, or seen the ugly intruder eating away my innocence day after day. You see, this dark world that had overtaken me, this horror that overwhelmed my life, had been a secret for almost two years—but the tip of this monster was about to emerge after months of hiding.

From Darkness to Light

October 19, 2002, started out as any other Saturday, which at the Cherry house, meant schoolwork, chores, and on this Saturday, preparing for our upcoming trip to Tulsa. I awoke and began my daily tasks as normal, carefully masking the battle raging in my inner being until 5:00 p.m. when I received a phone call from my dad. My heart began beating rapidly for I had recently grown very fearful of my father, the man I had once adored. After having been Daddy's dear "K-Baby" for so long, I had been pushing him away from my heart. I was terrified that he would find out my secret one day and discover the dishonesty I had been living in for so long. I was unaware that today would be the day that my darkness, lies, and shame were all exposed and brought to light.

The next few hours became a blur, for as soon as I realized what was happening, my mind began to panic and shut down to everything around me. My father had just discovered a large cell phone bill indicating that someone from our household had been calling a forty-six-year-old man from my dad's congregation every night for weeks. He believed it was a mistake—yet this definitely was not a mistake, but rather the beginning of an ugly unveiling of my hidden life. The truth was this closet affair wasn't new but had been occurring on and off for nearly two years.

Living this secret life had become the norm for me: putting on a good girl front in the day, and sneaking around in the night. Living a double life, however, was not what I desired. I had been tricked, taken, used—my innocence snatched away. Through this man, my heart had been stolen, my mind confused, and my spirit crushed. Still in some way, the sickening attention had felt reassuring.

For many months I had been placing phone calls in the middle of the night to this man with whom I thought I had found love and acceptance. In my naivety, I never doubted his intentions and by the time they were clear, I was already too entangled to walk away. Talking for long hours every night had recently become the norm. Yet I didn't understand why he was no longer speaking of innocent things but was now speaking of my body as an amusement park, seemingly perfect for his sexual gratification.

Entangled and Awestruck

How did I find myself entangled in such a horrible, strange mess? I remember clearly the spring of 2000 when a new family began attending our growing church. I immediately took a strong liking to these people. They were outgoing, talented, and passionate after God, and I was young, tender, and impressionable. This middle-aged couple's twenty-one-year-old son was exemplary in character, traveling in youth ministry circles that I admired. I looked up to him and wanted to imitate his devotion to the things of God—even to the point of having a childlike crush on him. The wife was kind and caring to all she came in contact with. She was gifted in children's ministry and served at our church with creativity and dedication. She seemed motherly and committed. The man was a very talented musician who served on our church's worship team with my mom (the worship leader), my older brother (our keyboard player), and me (a singer), and was an incredible asset to our primitive band. Many said this man was a musical genius, and his talents were highly sought out. He was also a well-regarded, seasoned employee of a local Christian organization. All in all, these people were friendly and loyal, demonstrating qualities I had already witnessed the lack of in so many just in the short time my family had been in ministry. Needless to say, I was awestruck.

We had gladly welcomed this family not only into our church, but into our lives as family friends. We visited in their home for cookouts and gatherings and hosted them in our home for church events and practices. It was well known that this family had been through some serious relationship problems, but these issues seemed a thing of the past, having been confronted and dealt with before. It appeared that God had indeed redeemed them from past weaknesses and problems. Besides, helping people get healed from their problems was part of our family's and our church's job.

I thought no more about the history of these people, but rather, in a strange way became more and more connected to them. I tried desperately to make a good impression on them. I faithfully helped them set up their church equipment each week, and I was the first to jump to their aid in public or private. I felt they were a part of me, companions that would always be there.

As time passed, changes began to take place in this family, thus affecting me also. The son moved to another state to attend college. Shortly after, the man and his wife experienced difficulties in their marriage and separated. By this time, I was strongly attached to them and felt personally hurt by these changes. The only member of this family that was left in town was the man.

From the beginning he carried an odd air about him, an air that seemed at times intimidating, but always inviting. He appeared to keep mostly to himself, but was always ready to give a smile or a wink to me. He had long since paid me special attention in soft, subtle ways. I had felt for some time that we had a special friendship. He would often compliment my singing ability, servitude, or appearance, which didn't seem to bother his wife or son, so I just took it as a normal part of being friends with the family. I felt like my hard work to impress this family was paying off! While it may have occurred to me that it was strange to receive such attention from a man 31 years my senior, I brushed aside any concern and took it as though it was normal. After all, I reasoned, there wasn't anything overtly inappropriate about it—just a hug here, a whispered "I love you" there, or an occasional comment about my beautiful smile or hair.

It was only after these changes in this family took place that this man began to carry on an increasing amount with me. It was also during this time that he began traveling more for his work. One thing led to another and soon he and I were chatting online multiple nights a week after he introduced me to the instant message world available on the Internet. Soon, he was not just saying hello and goodbye, but was asking me when I would be online, and when we could chat again.

Eventually he introduced me to the concept of a live webcam, which I requested for Christmas, saying that way we could see each other while we talked. Next came the comments he made while he watched me on the web camera, not dirty remarks, but subtle changes, so as to dull my senses to his real intentions. Comments about church events and his work schedule became comments about my hair and body, how he missed me, how he wanted to see me and hug me. His remarks at times made me feel a bit queasy, but by this time I was hooked.

In January of 2002, my dad stumbled upon some online discussions that had taken place between us. He was very alarmed that we had been corresponding, but he knew little to nothing of the context of our discussion or the frequency of it. Assuming there was no real problem, but still wanting to be cautious, my dad ordered me to stop all personal contact with this man immediately. His reaction startled me, and though reluctant, I obeyed. But the hook had already been set and the strange pull inside me toward this man only grew.

Though the threat on my life from this man appeared gone, it was really only crouching at the door waiting to devour me. During the spring months of 2002, interactions between the two of us were very brief, and somewhat rare, only taking place when this man was in town attending church. But in July of 2002, I called him along with a list of other people about a church event, and the crouching issue became life size. He told me that he missed talking to me, and asked me to call him again. I felt torn, but the decision at hand had in many ways already been made. The pull was strong, and I gave in. I was already emotionally involved and there was no turning back now. Little did I know what was waiting for me just around the corner.

Living a Double Life

Looking back, I remember being utterly consumed with thoughts about this man. My desire to please him, impress him, and be loyal to him dominated my life. I know that this devastating connection must have been constructed on a spiritual level because the tie was so strange and strong it could not have simply occurred in the natural realm.

I now had the difficult task of splitting my life. I had to keep up my performance in all areas of my outer life, yet find ways to secretly talk to this man who told me he needed me. I came up with creative solutions: I would go grocery shopping for Mom and call him from a payphone or ask to make a phone call at someone else's house and go to a back bedroom. My conversations with him were soon becoming more frequent and lasting longer. He continued to ask me to call him, and provided additional ways for me to get in contact with him. He began giving me calling card numbers so that when he was out of town, I could make the long distance calls discreetly. For weeks this relationship grew, and with each passing day so did the weight of confusion and guilt that I felt.

When I resumed school in August 2002, I became even more stressed to manage my schoolwork while carrying on this secret relationship that was consuming more and more of my time. As I felt overtaken by shame, I began overachieving in all outward areas of my life. I was excelling at an unbelievable rate in school and church activities, subconsciously working extra hard on the outside since I felt so very rotten on the inside.

As the weeks passed, the conversations between this man and me became much more personal. Through the summer of 2002, I saw this man at church only a handful of times as he was traveling extensively for work purposes. Yet, whether in or out of town, our phone conversations were still occurring multiple times per week; and the few times I did see him, our one-on-one interactions were intensified. These changes included secret hugging, kissing on the cheek and hands, and tender words exchanged.

By September 2002, I was completely consumed with this relationship. The man was out of town again, and was begging me to keep calling him, but I was running out of logical options. I lost all common sense and began stealing my dad's cell phone to make the calls, now escaping to our outdoor garage to carry on our discussions. At first these were daytime calls, but soon became frequent in the middle of the night. My life became even more complicated as I struggled to put on a nice front each day and stay awake long hours each night. As I lay on the cold floor of our outdoor garage night after night, I listened to the graphic sexual discussions of this man, unsure of how to respond. I felt sickened, yet my heart was with him, for I had come to love him deeply—or so I thought.

I grew increasingly confused, yet controlled by the very thing that deceived me. My perception had become warped and my judgment twisted. I could no longer think rationally or reason with common sense. My thoughts were spent figuring ways that I could secretly spend more time with my admirer. He warned me to keep quiet about our "love," and I kept my mouth shut. Since he told me that people would be mad at me if they found out, I didn't dare speak a word. I also knew that he would be in trouble if anyone discovered what we were doing, and I felt it my duty to protect him. So I planned how we could continue to speak in secret, perhaps meet in secret, and in the future live life together in secret. All of my thoughts, decisions, and actions were based on this growing obsession.

This addiction controlled my very life, but what was I addicted to? Was I just a rebel, seeking to wreak havoc in my parent's lives? Was I a sexual pervert, looking for attention to gratify my desires? Or was I just a girl, who, in the difficult season of the teenage years, stepped off the path of righteousness and reached out for a counterfeit form of acceptance? I had fallen in a pit way over my head, and it was beyond my ability to climb out. Unable to escape the cycle of excitement, guilt, pleasure, and deception that tormented me I felt trapped—not just by a person, but by the powers of darkness seeking to destroy my life. I was torn. I had seemingly found the acceptance my teenage heart so desired, but with it came the devastating effects of sexual abuse day after day.

I lived in a fantasyland within my own mind. Whenever my thoughts wandered into reality, I felt trapped in a predicament with no way out. I only saw two options—confess to my parents what was going on or stay in the relationship. Both options had devastating ends, and I knew it. Often playing out each one in my mind made me feel like I could live through neither so I denied both, slipping back into my fantasy world as quickly as possible.

I learned to pretend as though I enjoyed the sexual exploration and desires communicated to me by this much older man. Terrified of losing his "love," I went along with all of his perverted ideas, even when they made me feel filthy, violated, and used. I believed the lie that he needed me to meet these needs in his life lest he be lonely and miserable. He said that he loved me, and I felt appreciated. Swearing my devotion to him and him alone, I obeyed whatever he said for me to do.

Every night, he reminded me of all that he would do for me—
come after me, marry me, and love me.

This perverted man had found a way into my young life,
shattered my values, and convinced me to believe his sick lies.
Yet instead of running from him, I ran to him night after
night, giving him my fragile heart and all my trust. I was no
longer my own, but I was possessed by this horrific monster
whose manipulation had overtaken my life.

This was my secret hidden from the world, the source of
my secret pleasure and my inner turmoil. I would do anything
to keep it from being exposed, yet deep down I longed desper-
ately for someone to detect it and pull me out of this sinking
pit. Even though I had been brainwashed into believing this
relationship was normal and acceptable, I felt the pain that
this deep violation brought with it. But I was confused about
the source of the pain. My thoughts were blurred—was I really
just hurting myself? After all, I was the, "black sheep of the
family," he said. Perhaps my family was the enemy. They
would no doubt reject me if they found out about my "love."

As this abusive relationship formed, my heart had been
drawn away from God and away from the safety of my
parents' protection. I had drifted from what I knew to be true.
Consequently, I had felt heightened awareness to the changes
and pressures of the world. As I grew older the temptation to
rebel knocked on my door. In my weakness, though, I hadn't
turned to the acceptance of my parents, or to the true love of
my heavenly Father, but to the cheap counterfeit which sucked
the very life from me—spirit, soul, and body.

Was it only a man controlling me? No, the force that held me no man could establish or break in his own strength. I had opened the door for principalities and powers of darkness [see Eph. 6:12], and I would pay dearly.

Payday came sooner than I expected. Could it be real? Surely I hadn't been found out. It must be a dream! Was there no escaping the disturbing reality? On October 19 it was indeed real, and after hours of lying and fighting the onset of truth, I finally confessed to the forbidden relationship.

The Aftershock of Exposure

That Saturday night in October was the longest of my life. While the investigation of the situation was made, my parents looked on in horror, as I became a different person before their very eyes. I cried out in panic and outrage, begging them to leave this relationship undisturbed. My parents watched in dread as I professed my love and devotion to my perpetrator. My undercover life had been exposed and the misery and confusion that followed were indescribable. An intense battle raged on that seemed to be a battle between my parents and me, but in reality, this battle waged between truth and deception. Holding fast to my abused way of thinking, I refused to move off of my pedestal of lies. Instead, the hours crawled by in confusion, anguish, and misery.

Sleep couldn't bring me comfort that night. Long hours were spent seeking truth and looking for a quick fix. This, however, was a problem that had developed over a long period of time and would take even longer to mend. I groped about in mental darkness and confusion, looking for comfort, but finding none. My head heavy, my eyes swollen from tears, I only wanted relief, but it was not soon in coming.

Over the next few days my behavior changed drastically. October 19 marked the beginning of a downward spiral that continued for many months. I didn't understand what was taking place. I only knew that I was drowning in a sea of suffering and anguish that I had never before deemed possible. I strangely believed that my life had been ruined since my "soul mate" had been taken away. How could I carry on without him?

In truth, I had been abused, defiled, defamed, and damaged beyond my ability to cope. After having been the object of a man's sexual perversion and mania, I was left with an utterly broken heart and a crushed spirit and soul. Yet only over a period of many months of horror, pain, and confusion, would I or anyone else even begin to understand the real story of what had happened to me.

The next few weeks I lived in utter torment. I quit eating and shut down my life, hoping that it would simply end. I lived out my misery under stacks of blankets in my room with the door locked, the light off, and the window covered. For this period of time, I proceeded to live in seclusion and alienation from everything and everyone, refusing and unable to face reality. I fell into very deep depression. I slept most of the time, since sleep allowed me to momentarily escape the grief that shook my being. But even when I slept, my mind was filled with terrifying nightmares that often caused me to shake with fear. In these nightmares, my mind wandered to many circumstances, some real and some imagined, but all equally horrifying.

Often I awoke from sleeping all day, only to feel more hopeless than before. My iniquity and pain were more than I could bear. The only prayers I prayed during this time were prayers of fury, begging God to take my life. I wept regularly until my eyes had no more tears to cry and my body had no strength left to sob. The sorrow I felt weighed down my body, soul, and spirit, just as if I was carrying a load impossible to bear. This load was very real—a load of guilt, pain, regret, and anger.

I quickly became numb to everything around me— both physically and emotionally. I didn't have the strength to care what happened. I felt I had been hurt beyond the pain any other person could ever inflict and relied heavily on coping mechanisms to continue in my existence. Fantasy, anger, denial, and cruelty were a few of the regulars I used to conceal my inner pain and distract myself from the reality of my disgusting life. Occasionally, I wandered away from home for a day, leaving without notifying anyone. I would find a place of solitude, weep until I had no strength left to cry, then lay down on the frosted ground and sleep. I no longer felt the hunger pains in my stomach or the freezing cold on my skin. I only felt the desperation in my soul.

Very soon after this nightmare began, I isolated myself in my own world where no one else was welcome. I withdrew both physically and emotionally. Much like a wounded animal, I secluded myself from the outside world, building strong walls, and allowing no one entrance to my heart and soul. I found it more difficult, however, to keep intruders out of my physical surroundings. I dwelt in my own bedroom, emerging only when forced to, and usually after a battle.

Whenever I was literally dragged out of the house to eat, go to church, or see a counselor, it was only after an intense struggle. Even then, I no longer cared what any person thought about me.

I didn't attempt to mask my pain, so I often walked around with an angry expression, sobbed openly, or just lay down in public places like the benches in the hallways of church. When I did emerge from my dark chamber, I usually acted as if no one was present, completely ignoring any remarks, questions, or comments from anyone in my household. I was cruel and ruthless to every member of my family, acting almost inhuman to them. When I did speak, it was only with outbursts of violent screaming and accusation. I was voicing my anger toward my parents, my life, and my God. I held fast to the lies that my perpetrator had sown into my brain, refusing to believe anything rational.

My father and mother did not know where to turn. I pretended to enjoy making their lives miserable, but deep down I despised myself for it. At times I didn't understand why I behaved as I did. Feeling as though a force beyond myself controlled me, I submitted to it, seeing no better option. I was exploding with anger that had to be directed at someone. The target became my parents, the very people laying down their lives in a desperate attempt to save me, their dying little girl.

They tried everything they believed might restore me. Never willing to give up, they prayed, wept, took me on vacations, gave me gifts, and showed me their love every way they knew how. But they were colliding with a wall that seemed to be growing thicker by the day. Taking me to counselors and psychologists only appeared to strengthen the barrier between my parents and me. Many times they considered homes, shelters, and mental hospitals, looking for anything that would bring me back to reality. Despite all of their efforts, I appeared to be growing worse every day.

Throughout this time, I made several feeble suicide attempts, but these only made me feel emptier. I did find some relief in self-mutilation. Punishing myself felt good. I found that if my physical body was hurting, I could momentarily forget my emotional suffering. I made a regular practice of cutting my arms and legs, making sure that I suffered intense pain. I knew that I was only damaging myself further, but I didn't care.

My secret issue was no longer just my problem at all. I was now hurting my family, as well as everyone around me, but not because I desired to. I felt rejected beyond restoration and wounded beyond repair. Having been brainwashed into believing that I was a destructive person, I acted like one, destroying everything within my reach.

Now severely depressed, confused, and hopeless, I had no desire to go on. I had fallen too far, lost my reason for living, and turned my back on God. Having given up on everything in my life, I surrendered to the torment that knocked at my door.

The girl who had once been full of life, joy, and hope for the future was now lost. After believing that I was invincible, I had now been invaded and destroyed. The same person who used to encourage others to never give up had now herself lost all hope. My life was now a pile of rubbish, useful for nothing. There was only one chance left for me—I needed a miracle.

CHAPTER 3

Blessed and Full of
Promise—the Early Years

*To give the full picture of the impact Kalyn's disclosure
and the aftereffects it had on us, I (Lisa) want to share
some of our personal background with you. I believe it
will shed light on who we were prior to that crisis and reveal
some earlier missteps—like my foolishness based on my ignorance of God's ways, my unrenewed mind, and my areas of
rebellion to His Word—that could have contributed to Kalyn
being so vulnerable to the perpetrator of the abuse.*

From the time I (Lisa) was a little girl, I had always
wanted to be a mother. In fact, I was known in my
neighborhood as being the last little girl to give up
playing with dolls. My own parents had demonstrated
well to my sister and me the joys of a loving, stable,
secure family life. So, I couldn't wait for my turn to be

the mommy. (I never dreamed what was ahead for me in that role!) Yet, I was also a product of the American generation of the late 1960s and '70s. I grew up singing a popular song that had become an anthem of the women's lib movement back then—"I Am Woman, Hear Me Roar"—and I intended to do some roaring.

As a teen, I knew that somewhere out there was that perfect career that would fulfill all my plans for success, and in my young mind I figured I could fit my perfect husband and my two perfectly spaced children around my perfectly achieving career, *perfectly*. I've often asked myself how this strong, liberated, well-educated, career-driven young woman of the 1980s became a full-time, home-educating mother of ten in the twenty-first century. My best explanation is that I had one plan and God had another—and I'm so glad His plan won!

It's not that I had never thought to ask God about my life plan when I was a youth. I remember asking Him regularly, but there were some limits I put on my asking. I had my own modern mindsets and paradigms and theories and reasonings, and I carefully tucked my Bible and my faith in around those new "liberated" viewpoints.

You may be thinking, *Ten children, home schooling, pastoring a church? This lady must be nuts!* Rest assured I can understand those concerns. In fact, when some innocent, naïve person approaches one of my children and asks, "Do you have any brothers or sisters?" my own child's answer tends to shock me, and I'm their mother! I do feel, though, that while my life may be unusual, it's not crazy but is incredibly blessed and full of promise. That's how I felt when I met Doug.

The Path to Ten

Doug and I met during my last months of high school in 1979. Within weeks of dating we were passionately in love, and I was quite sure he was *the one*. He was kind, smart, good-looking, successful, loving, athletic, articulate, strong, and liberated enough to let me be me. We seemed a perfect fit, and we met in a way that foreshadowed our future life calling together—he was leading his church youth group, and I was leading mine. We shared a strong love for God, but we had interesting differences in our spiritual views. Yet love is sometimes blind, or at least completely optimistic! I figured a few quick changes by me and Doug would surely see all spiritual, political, and life issues from my more liberated point of view.

After Doug completed his college degree in accounting, we were married at my home church. It was a fairy tale perfect wedding with a happy ending. Our life together was (and is still today) incredibly close, loving, wonderful, and satisfying. We lived near St. Louis, Missouri while I completed my undergraduate degree in nursing and Doug worked for Price Waterhouse in public accounting. When I finished college, however, I wasn't satisfied I'd made the correct career decision. Even as a young girl, I had sensed God's calling on my life toward pastoral ministry, so I changed direction and began making plans to pursue a master's degree at a St. Louis seminary to qualify me to become a local church pastor. Doug thought he had married a nurse, but now he was going to become a pastor's husband. Yet because he loved me, he made peace with being willing to fit his career of public accounting around my career of pastoring.

Back in 1983 we figured that since my career would be so demanding, it might be better to start the two perfectly spaced children process while I was finishing graduate school. At least I remember us claiming that was our reasoning, but I think the real truth was that I just wanted to have a baby. We look back now and thank God for that strong maternal drive that He had placed inside me.

Our first precious baby, Nathan, turned my world upside down. Sitting in the hospital holding my little miracle, I felt like my heart would burst with love and joy—and also like my mind would burst with confusion. I was now personally responsible for this human life and found all of my liberated, modern, career-minded, daycare planning views suddenly in question: Who was going to raise this child? Who would be the one to feed and love, change, and mold him? Could I really just hand him off to others when he was so young and innocent knowing that, unlike many women, I could choose to be at home? So I didn't return to my school commitments or my career; now full-time mothering would be my job. We moved back to our hometown in Illinois and quietly built our little family and Doug's financial services business.

My decision to stay at home was not easy. Since I had never planned to be at home and had previously developed quite a negative image about any woman who would "waste her brain as a full-time mom," I entered into quite a difficult self-searching struggle. I look back on those days as the wilderness years. When you put all of your life dreams and goals up on the rack for analysis, the larger questions of life just naturally begin to come to the surface: *Why am I here? What is my life purpose? Does God really have a personal plan for my family and for me?*

Remember, my faith understanding, doctrinal ideas, and whole worldview were built on my liberal mindset. So, when one piece of my liberal worldview (the role of women and mothers) came into question, it was like a ball of yarn began to unwind on the inside of me and everything became a tangled up mess. My confusion led to questioning—which is not necessarily a bad thing. God can use questions to eventually get us the answers we need.

The End of Self

In the midst of those questioning years, our precious little Kalyn arrived. Her appearance did much to solidify my growing viewpoint that mothering was indeed a noble profession of incredible importance. I poured my heart and life into being the best mother possible. I studied every modern book I could find on the subjects of breastfeeding newborns, caring for babies, taming toddlers, and teaching preschoolers. I was determined to raise up an emotionally healthy, successful next generation, and it didn't matter the personal sacrifice needed to achieve my goals.

On the other hand, I certainly wasn't sharpening my skills by consulting the Bible or other Christian authors. Doug and I were very active in our local church, but my personal faith was in a spiritual state of crisis and confusion. I found it easier to compartmentalize my life and keep my Sunday morning faith questions separated from my weekday childrearing questions.

While I was dwelling in a spiritual wilderness, Doug was growing closer to God and stronger in his personal faith, but during those years we had a very odd unspoken truce of silence. Thinking that he should pursue his own more "conservative, old-fashioned" faith ideas in his own personal way, and I should pursue my more "modern, enlightened, liberal" faith ideas in my own personal way, we each must have concluded it was safer just not to talk about "religion." I'm not sure how we didn't shipwreck our relationship back then, but somehow God protected us.

As the years rolled by, I would watch Doug get up early and go outside to pray. His Bible was his constant companion, and I watched his life grow more peaceful and steady and prosperous as he meditated constantly on God's Word. I watched him overcome a very serious season of mental anguish by growing in his faith. He talked of his personal relationship with Jesus with increasing excitement, and I found myself strangely jealous of his passion for God. I caught myself wondering, *Does he possibly have something that I don't have? Does he know something that I don't know?*

For years I learned to cast down those thoughts quickly and work harder to explain my logical, liberal viewpoint of the Bible and the world. I certainly didn't want to risk being persuaded to become what I disparagingly labeled as one of those "right-wing, Jesus-freak, evangelical Christian types." However, God was at work (I know from personal experience, He's always at work!)—He was working to bring me to the end of myself and my own foolish pride.

An Instant Kind of Change

After having thrown myself into mothering two children with such a passion, I begged Doug for a third opportunity at mothering. I actually decided it was a job I enjoyed, so we broke our two-child mold and daringly agreed on "just one more." Lucas arrived in 1991. When the euphoria of his birth waned, my spiritual wilderness turned into a spiritual desert. I was tired and weary on the inside. Even worse, some of my previously held viewpoints and arguments were causing me more questions than answers.

I had been trained in seminary to believe much of the Bible contained stories that could be useful for life instruction, but were not necessarily literally true or relevant for today. Teachings that said Adam and Eve and Jonah were probably mythical and not real historical people made me question the historical accuracy of Moses and Abraham and Joshua. I knew I had a real problem brewing when I began to have the same questions about the stories of the life of Jesus.

I had always believed in Jesus; I had asked Him into my heart as a child. Should I wonder about the truth of the stories of Jesus? Just how much of the Bible should I believe in? How was I going to determine which parts of the Bible were literary myth or culturally irrelevant? It seemed my Bible was more full of holes than answers, so I began to cry out to God for help in sorting out my mental, emotional, and spiritual confusion. As it turned out, that was all He had been waiting for me to do—to ask my questions with an authentic, desperate willingness to listen to His response.

His answer to me was quick and miraculous. After all those years of silence in our relationship, I remember the night I finally got up the courage to ask Doug to tell me his spiritual story. He did not, as I had feared, begin to lecture me about all my "wrong" beliefs. He simply shared with me his close, personal, intimate relationship with God and told me of the answers he found in God's Word for all the challenges of life's questions. I found myself truly wanting what he had. His heart overflowed with a love from our heavenly Father that I so desperately needed.

His story included an encounter with the third person of the Trinity named the Holy Spirit. I have to confess I didn't understand that part at all. Any discussion of the Holy Spirit (past mentioning him at the end of the doxology song we knew from church) seemed too primitive, uneducated, bizarre, and divisive for my tastes. I knew some of those folks I labeled unkindly as the "Holy Rollers" type, and I always prayed that Doug would stay far away from them. Now, come to find out, he'd been one of them for years!

That day in 1991 I knew that something in my stubborn and hostile heart was dramatically different. I didn't feel angered or even threatened by Doug's testimony as I usually did. I didn't argue or bristle. I suddenly was hungry for a real heart change. A new sense of hope rose up on the inside of me, and for the first time in my life, I was willing to step out of my intellectual comfort zone and ask God for something I couldn't yet understand. I remember praying something like, *Father, I don't understand what Doug is telling me about his personal relationship with You and with the Holy Spirit, but I can see that Your power is very evident in Doug's life. I know it doesn't seem to fit what I've ever believed, but whatever Doug has in his life, that's what I want.*

God honored the sincerity of a middle-of-the-night prayer that wasn't fancy or even doctrinally precise. See, God isn't particularly interested in our intellectual understanding or eloquence; He's interested in our humility. That night I wondered what would happen next as I lay there in my bed. To my disappointment, mixed with relief, nothing in my perceivable sensory realm appeared different, so I just drifted off to sleep.

When I awoke the next morning, however, my world was absolutely, completely different. Instantly, it was as if scales had fallen off my eyes. Something inside of me had unquestionably changed. Remember the experience that

Saul had in the book of Acts? He had been a religiously zealous Jew but was also a great persecutor of the church of Jesus Christ. When Saul encountered Jesus on that road to Damascus and completely surrendered his will and intellect to Him, all of Saul's ideas changed and his blind eyes were opened to truth. (Acts 9.) That was the instant kind of change that occurred in my life when I was spirit filled. When I picked up my Bible and read it that morning, it was amazingly alive—and suddenly I knew that I knew it was also *literally true*—all of it.

An incredible passion for God filled every cell of my being. I had given my life to Jesus as a child, but now through the power of the Holy Spirit, my relationship with Him was close and personal. My Father reached in and healed my hurting heart and all I wanted to do was make Him known to others. My life questions now had answers.

After that, like Doug, I was up early praying and reading my Bible. I was a totally different woman! My thoughts changed, my behaviors changed, and my beliefs most definitely changed. The very things I had ridiculed and persecuted Doug for believing all those years were now personally true for me. I no longer fought for my equal rights. I just wanted to give my rights away and serve the God I had grown to love.

Our marriage and home life immediately changed for the better. We were now both passionately intent on building every area of our lives on God's Word and His ways because we could so clearly see that every time we left our own way behind and went His way, healing, peace, joy, and order followed. Why would we ever want to go our own foolish way again? Life became an awesome, exciting adventure. People around us were being changed as we began to share our family story.

In Season and Out of Season

Not long after I was filled with the Holy Spirit God began to call Doug into full-time ministry. In fact, in 1993 He called us to move from Illinois to Tulsa for a season of ministry education. Ironically, Doug would be the one pursuing a graduate seminary education instead of me. The decision was not easy to move a growing family and a growing financial services business cross-country and begin a master's degree program. Yet we were absolutely confident that we were in the middle of God's will for our lives, and He would therefore take care of our needs.

During this season God began to talk to us about having another child. It really wasn't a discussion with Him about that but about who would be Lord over all of our womb decisions. What a scary thought! Yield to the Lord how many babies we would have? Even for a woman who loved babies, I liked the control over if, how, and when they would arrive; and I was sure we should be done having children. After all, we had a ministry calling and a season of education to fulfill. We felt that our baby season was surely over.

Nevertheless, by this time in our walk with the Lord, we had learned to trust that His ways were always higher and more wonderful than ours, so little Rebekah joined our family. With each precious little baby thereafter, both Doug and I would hear those familiar words of comfort from our heavenly Father down deep in our hearts saying, "Will you trust Me to give you the blessing of yet another child?" and each time our answer to Him would be yes! So over the years we embarked on a remarkable journey of raising Nathan, Kalyn, Lucas, Rebekah, Hannah, Micah, Matthew, Ethan, and Lydia, and later Josiah in a two-child-per-family norm world.

God had truly stretched out our hearts as He had stretched out our faith. He had granted us abundant prosperity in the fruit of our womb as is talked about in the great blessing chapter of the Bible, Deuteronomy 28. Along with every precious gift of a baby, He brought us more health, strength, provision, wisdom, order, and grace—miraculously, abundantly, graciously. So I can clearly say that somehow, ten healthy pregnancies later, I am physically stronger than ever and more certain of God's incredible, amazing power.

Even as the babies continued to arrive, God supported us by prospering Doug's financial services business while we lived in Tulsa. During our five-year season there, Doug completed his master's degree in theology from Oral Roberts University, and we began to teach classes at our home church's Bible school, Victory Bible Institute. As we sensed God's plans to eventually launch our whole family into His full-time service, we thought Tulsa would be our permanent ministry home. But, once again, the Lord had different plans. He called us back to our hometown of

Carbondale, Illinois, in 1998 to begin a new church called Victory Christian Center of Southern Illinois.

Church pioneering proved to be a greater adventure than we had ever imagined. As we started our church in our living room with three families, each of our children began to rise up at young ages and share in the work of the ministry. It was not an easy lifestyle, but we were strong as a family, unified in vision, and passionate about fulfilling our adventurous calling together.

As the years passed, our young church encountered some resistance and difficulties, but the joys far outweighed them and the church steadily grew and matured. Faithful and committed Christian families began to join us in our mission to reach out to a hurting world and perform our vision to "Take Back Ground and Build Frontline Families." We saw God's miraculous hand of provision at every turn, and we were confident and optimistic about our future in family ministry.

So with all this miraculous power of God flowing in our lives, through every season of change and growth, why could we not find any instant miracle power on the horrible evening of October 19, 2002? As our story turns out, His miraculous power would only be manifested on the other side of that dark night.

CHAPTER 4

The Dark Night

"It's a dark night, a dark hour."

LUKE 22:53 MSG

"It was the best of times, it was the worst of times"[1]—
that famous first line of a well-known literary classic
truly captured this season of my life best. While
much more challenging now, it was still the best of times
helping Doug pastor a growing church and raise our
wonderful brood. Being the mother of nine children (at
that time) I had known about mothering valleys; I had
weathered enough tough stages, strange habits, stomach
flu, morning sickness, and sibling rivalries to be able to
trust God to eventually bring us back up to level ground
again. Yet I was unprepared for the relentless force of "the
worst of times" that suddenly came upon us—the dark
night of our parenting crisis with Kalyn.

After we discovered Kalyn's sexual abuse, it was a
horrible time when my mind became utterly exhausted

searching for answers to a problem far too complicated for it to solve. It was a season of time when my own failings and inadequacies were so magnified that they looked insurmountable and hopeless. It was a time of great temptation to give up, give in, or give back. It was a journey with time urgency, for a child's life was at stake. It was a time I now call "the dark night of a mother's soul," but before October 19, 2002, I never knew "the dark night" existed.

The phrase "the dark night of the soul" is recorded as far back as the 1500s, written about in a book by that title. Perhaps it is just some overworked poetic phrase used to describe a really tough spot in life, but I can't think of a better way to explain something that I believe to be of life and death importance to parents. So we're going to look at each of the main words in this phrase because for people who aren't able to navigate a dark night, destruction and defeat can result; but those who are able to properly handle and navigate through a dark night can find life and victory in their battle.

"Dark"

At the very opening act of creation, God talked about darkness. "God said: 'Let there be *light*,' and there was light. God saw that the *light* was *good*, and He separated the light from the *darkness*. God called the light 'day,' and the darkness he called 'night'" (Gen. 1:3–5). Throughout His Word, God identified Himself as the God who is light as in 1 John 1:5 that says, "God is light; in Him there is no darkness at all." And Jesus himself declared, "I am the light of the world" (John 8:12).

Yet just as God the Father, God the Son, God the Holy Spirit (1 John 5:7–8 NKJV), and the entire heavenly host are considered light, there is another who is deemed spiritual darkness and described in Scripture as the worker of darkness—Satan, the devil, and his workers, the demons. In fact, in several verses his deeds are termed "deeds of darkness" (Rom. 13:12; Eph. 5:11). Deeds and acts of darkness simply *cannot* come from God.

> Don't be deceived, my dear brothers. Every good gift and perfect gift is from above, coming down from the Father of the heavenly lights, who does not change like shifting shadows.

> James 1:16,17

I like the way this passage is explained in *John Gill's Exposition of the Entire Bible*: "God...is light itself, and in him is no darkness at all...wherefore he being holy, cannot turn to that which is evil; nor can he, who is the fountain of light, be the cause of darkness...since every good and perfect gift comes from him, evil cannot proceed from him, nor can he tempt any to it."[2] So the instigator of deeds of darkness is the one Jesus calls the thief, who comes to steal, kill, and destroy. (John 10:10.)

We are living in times of an incredible spiritual battle between the forces of light and the forces of darkness. "This is no afternoon athletic contest that we'll walk away from and forget about in a couple of hours," the *Message Bible* tells us. "This is for keeps, a life-or-death fight to the finish against the Devil and all his angels" (Eph. 6:12 MSG). In other words, it is a battle between good and evil; righteousness and sin; truth and deception; life and death. All we have to do to see the reality of it is to look around us.

Every human being is operating center stage in the midst of this battle. That's why Jesus, when asked how we should pray, closed His prayer with, "deliver us from evil" (Matt. 6:13 KJV). "The meaning here" says Albert Barnes in his Bible commentary, "is, 'deliver us from [Satan's] power, his snares, his arts, his temptations.' He is supposed to be the great parent of evil, and to be delivered from him is to be safe."[3]

There's protection and safety with God (see Ps. 12:7; Prov. 18:10; 1 John 5:18), but the world, as our kids know it, is a much tougher, unsafe place than we knew it, even one generation ago. As we keep moving closer to the end of this present age and Jesus' prophesied return to the earth (see Matt. 28:20; Luke 21:27), the battle for our lives and the lives of our children is growing more intense. Jesus spoke of this increase in wickedness and conflict in Matthew 24, and it is happening before our eyes daily.

Ron Luce, a seasoned youth ministry expert and founder of Teen Mania, presents these disturbing statistics regarding our teenagers in *Battle Cry for a Generation*:

✗ 1 out of 11 attempt *suicide* each year

✗ 40 percent have experimented with *self-injury* (are "cutters")

✗ 1 in 10 high school females have reported being *raped* at some point in their life

✗ 48 percent of high school seniors are *sexually active* (had sexual intercourse in past 3 months)

✗ 91 percent say there is no *absolute truth*

✗ 75 percent believe the central message of the Bible is "God helps those who help themselves"

✗ 1 in 5 children ages 10—17 who regularly use the Internet have received a sexual solicitation while online

✗ Every day, 8,000 teenagers in the United States become infected by an STD[4]

Another expert, the Centers for Disease Control and Prevention (CDC), estimates that 1-in-4 girls and 1-in-6 boys will be *sexually abused* by the age of 18.[5]

As Luce has sounded the battle cry across this land to save our young generation, he often describes the staggering effects the media has on our children's thoughts, beliefs, and actions. In another of his books, *Recreate,* he says, "It's no secret that teens are in trouble today. Hardly a week goes by in which we don't see headlines about teens destroying their or others' lives. We see the effects of perverse rock and hip-hop music, but we don't know what to do. We know that Hollywood and MTV have a grip on our kids, but we have no idea how to protect them. Even good God-fearing parents are seeing their children affected by this culture of destruction."[6]

Our family's crisis was not an isolated destructive incident, *and it did not come from God.* It wasn't by Him, and it wasn't His will for our family—even though now we are able to see good coming out of the pain of this tragedy. God does not work His plan on the earth by causing sin, perversity, and evil deeds. He is a good God who is perfect, holy, and without sin. He doesn't cause people to sin to accomplish His will.

Many people have been confused and have labeled such disastrous events in life as sovereign acts of God sent to teach us lessons and drive us toward Him. James, the brother of Jesus, makes this point very clear: "When tempted, no one should say, 'God is tempting me.' For God cannot be tempted by evil, nor does he tempt anyone; but each one is tempted when, by his own evil desire, he is dragged away and enticed. Then, after desire has conceived, it gives birth to sin; and sin, when it is full-grown, gives birth to death" (James 1:13–15).

One reason it's important to understand the source of the dark night is that when darkness tries to invade your home, many competing voices of explanation can be heard all around you. To avoid all confusion, remember that:

✓ Our God is a good and holy God.

✓ The dark night is an encounter with the spiritual forces of darkness at work on the earth today.

✓ The enemies in this battle are really not the *people* involved in the dark acts, but the forces of evil which have taken them captive to do their will for this season. (Eph. 6:12.)

✓ Darkness tries to bring fear.

✓ Darkness tries to overwhelm your senses.

✓ Darkness tries to hide its true origin so that you will be tempted to believe it doesn't even exist.

✓ Darkness can be shockingly dark.

✓ Whenever you FEEL LIKE, "Surely the darkness shall cover me;" you can be sure that, "even the night shall be light about [you]" (Ps. 139:11 KJV).

"Night"

We all know that *night* is a period of time that is opposite day. It is the cycle in which natural darkness rules. However, natural darkness can always be overruled by the introduction of artificial light. For instance, if a candle or flashlight can illuminate a field of darkness, then even though the natural force of night is darkness, *light always triumphs over darkness.* So, the dark *night* of the mother's soul is a period of time in which spiritual darkness is trying to rule and dominate.

We can see this in one translation of the original Hebrew word for *darkness,* which is, "persons in whom darkness...holds sway [control, influence, authority]."[7] But, night's dominance must always have its end when the sun's light overpowers it. So it is with the spiritual dark night of the soul. The introduction of enough spiritual light will force the end of night's season of dominance. (See Ps. 139:11.) That involves getting into God's presence and filling ourselves with His Word, which dispels the darkness.

"Mother's"

How do we define the term *mother*? One meaning of the Hebrew word for *mother* suggests "the bond of the family,"[8] but simply stated, the mother is the one who carries and births forth the new life of a child. In a more complete sense, a mother is one commissioned and entrusted by God to nurture and care for the next generation of young. A mother can acquire her charge by means of birth, adoption, or legal guardianship, but however this relationship is initiated, it is honored by God as a sacred trust of the heart.

Mothering is a uniquely feminine activity not to be confused with fathering. It is compassionate and gentle (1 Thess. 2:7), instructive and fervent. It has a loyalty of heart towards a child, which cannot be easily matched by any other human relationship. So as a mother, I have entitled my phrase "the dark night of the *mother's* soul" because I know it firsthand. Doug also went through his dark night of the soul, which would be called "the dark night of a father's soul." There is a difference. Doug will talk briefly about his dark night experience at the end of this book because couples involved in the dark night need to understand their differences. Both experiences are uniquely painful.

"Soul"

As the details of creation unfold in the book of Genesis, God reveals that He created us in His image. (Gen. 1:26.) Just as God is a three-part being—Father, Son, and Holy Spirit—He created man and woman as three-part beings: spirit, soul, and body. (1 John 5:7–8 NKJV; 1 Thess. 5:23.) Our *spirit* is that part of us that lives eternally after death. Our *body* is that part of us that we can see and touch. Our *soul* is a little harder to define for it is made up of the mind (our "thinker"), the emotions (our "feeler"), and the will (our "chooser").[9] So, a battle rages between all three of these parts when our soul is in a dark night. The *thinker* is in battle with the *feeler* and vice versa and the *chooser* is desperately trying to referee and make right choices. Unfortunately, the deeper the battle, the more difficult the choices.

Our souls are uniquely formed in us by God as He fashions us in the womb. (See Jer. 1:5.) The soul will, of course, be further influenced after birth by our life learning and experiences. God is infinitely creative, and no two "souls" are created alike. Because of this, every soul will respond uniquely to life's joys, questions, and challenges.

The bottom line is *the dark night of a mother's soul* can be defined as:

> A season of time when the mind, will, and emotions of a mother are in an incredible battle with darkness because of her role of mothering a child.

Diagnosis and Plans

As you can imagine, over the years I've read many books on mothering and on birth. You might say I've had more than the average amount of interest in the subjects! I always chuckle at some of the information certain books and well-intentioned Lamaze childbirth instructors give, particularly the ones who attempt to describe a labor contraction by instructing the father to squeeze hard the leg of the mother to mimic the labor intensity. That's the naïve image I took in to my first labor experience.

I arrived at the hospital that day not really sure whether I was in labor or not. I can clearly tell you after ten births that if you have to ask someone if you're in active labor, you're probably not. The warm smile and comforting words of an experienced birthing mother who says to a first-time mom, "You'll know when it's real labor," are so very true. Similarly, if you or someone you care about is in a dark night of the soul, I assure you, you'll know!

The dark night of the soul may be thought of as a second labor in the life of a child. It is not to be wished for or desired, but neither is it to be ignored or feared. It is not an inevitable part of every child's experience (thank God), but it can be experienced as the result of a fallen, tribulating, difficult world.

No one ever plans on experiencing a dark night of the soul, just as no one ever plans to experience a heart attack. A prudent response to the threat of heart disease is the practice of basic cardiac preventative care techniques coupled with pre-planned emergency response such as CPR and emergency medical assistance. This too is the case when bringing up children in these difficult times— a proper amount of "darkness attack prevention" must be matched with "emergency spiritual response plans."

Oh, how I wish I had been better prepared for our attack! How much needless extra emotional pain I bore. How much needless extra pain I inflicted. How differently I would have responded! The intensity of that dark night of *this* mother's soul was almost unbearable.

After Kalyn's shocking disclosure, the dark night I entered was like nothing I had ever before experienced. It was an utterly private world in my mind and heart where my emotions and senses became so pained and raw they could no longer be trusted. If I were to draw a picture of the dark night of my soul, it would be a circle surrounded by six emotions—anger, guilt, embarrassment, mourning, helplessness, and fear. I remember that sometimes I could travel my circle of soul torment in a matter of minutes, or sometimes I would linger in the different stages for days. But, for many months I lived in a vicious cycle of pain, unable to break out into the daylight.

Hot, passionate anger rose up in me like a wellspring of death. Some of it seemed to be primitive anger like the kind a mother bear exhibits with her cub. Some of the anger seemed much more complicated. I was so very angry at the family friend who perpetrated the sexual abuse. But, I was also angry at the unfairness of the situation I now found myself in of having to deal with a crime's aftermath of mental illness. I was angry at the loss of control over my own life. I was angry at Kalyn for the wrong choices she had made that had made her more vulnerable to the attack on her life. I was angry that daily life was now so complicated and difficult. I was angry at the forces of darkness for attacking my child. All of those angers seemed at least understandable, if not justifiable.

What about the irrational angers that my mind couldn't justify, like the anger I felt toward Doug when he couldn't convince Kalyn of the truth of her situation or control her defiant behavior. Or the anger I felt at others who made helpful suggestions about what we should do to "snap Kalyn out" of the rebellion and depression. Or the anger I felt at Kalyn for being so out of control and miserable. Or the anger that spilled over at my other children just because they were acting like kids. It was a daily battle of willing myself to forgive others, and it was exhausting work that left me raw and worn out.

On days I lost the anger battle, I would easily cycle into one of my many versions of guilt. Guilt for feeling angry. Guilt for acting angry. Guilt for what I thought I hadn't done to protect Kalyn from this attack. Guilt for all the ways I thought I had failed to mother Kalyn over the years. Guilt for all the ways I had failed to mother all my other children over the years. Guilt for not recognizing the warning signs of the abuse. Guilt for not giving the other kids the emotional support they needed during this crisis. Guilt for not being a better wife and doing more to relieve Doug's pain. Guilt, guilt, guilt!

Then embarrassment *and* shame *over our family's current status would rear its ugly head. I was so embarrassed to be living our problems in the public light that sometimes I wanted to run and hide. I was embarrassed that we couldn't control Kalyn's sudden change of behaviors, nor could we even explain them to very many people around us, as she was not ready for the sexual abuse issue to be made public. I was embarrassed that I, who was normally the counselor to others, became the one needing a counselor. I was ashamed of my weak performance and failures in other areas as projects and appointments would just slip my mind or seem insurmountable to accomplish.*

The anger, guilt, and embarrassment would then remind me of all the losses we had incurred as a family. A deep mourning—not just a sadness—but a sobbing kind of mourning would grip my emotions. Mourning over Kalyn's lost innocence. Mourning over lost relationship with her. Mourning over dreams and visions for our family life together. Mourning over lost finances and lost business and ministry opportunities.

When we missed Kalyn at the dinner table or when we couldn't pull her out of her room, my heart would grieve for her as if she were lost. When sometimes the children would forget to set a place for her at the table (since for weeks on end she would usually be unable to come), my chest would feel crushed under a weight of grief. When Kalyn ignored the children or refused to ever hold baby Lydia, my eyes would fill with tears.

A mother's highest job is to care for the needs of her family. I wanted so badly to fix this whole mess for everyone that when weeks stretched into months with no answers, relief, or breakthroughs, I was overwhelmed with a sense of helplessness. I was tempted to throw up my hands and quit, but where could a mother of nine (back then) go to quit? I knew that wasn't really possible so my mind began to contemplate at least quitting my work in ministry. Perhaps, I reasoned, I was no longer qualified for that anyway.

Self-doubts attacked my mind and I began to lose confidence in making normal, everyday parenting decisions. I felt that if I couldn't prevent or solve Kalyn's problem, how could I help the other kids solve their problems and grow up normally? What if this crisis was really a symptom of some potentially serious parenting flaw in me that would be passed on to my other children?

I remember in one particularly difficult moment, when my emotions were out of control, I told Doug that perhaps he had better find someone else to raise our kids since I obviously was failing Kalyn so terribly. Thank God for a husband who could listen to my heart's pain and yet not take me serious at my words! But by that point every area of life started to seem overwhelming, like when I would sometimes stand in an aisle at the grocery store unable to confidently decide which cereal was best to buy. My mind was overworked and tired of too much data, too little sleep, and too much reasoning.

Stuck in the Dark Night

Fear too seemed ever crouching at my door. Fear that I wouldn't be able to hold up to the mental and emotional pressures. Fear that we would never see our real Kalyn again or that she would run away from us and live a rebellious, *dangerous lifestyle. Fear that she would seriously hurt herself or get worse and require hospitalization. I'd often wake up at night with nightmares about all kinds of awful destructions. I would lay in bed unable to go back to sleep until I could sneak up to her room and check on her.*

Most of my fears were, unfortunately, justified. It wasn't the "boogey man" kind of fear that is easier to chalk up to an overactive imagination. We had real alarming things happening all around us. A girl that has been sexually abused often attempts to deal with her inward pain by what's called "acting out" behavior. Kalyn's dress became very provocative and her demeanor flirtatious and rebellious. Coupled with her obvious physical beauty, she was attracting quite a crowd of the wrong kind. It was like she was wearing a sign that read "every wounded, hurting, rebellious person welcome here." She was weak and incredibly impressionable and seemed amazingly oblivious to how dangerous many of these people were. We had to become her safety system, which she greatly resented. Every time the phone would ring for her, or I saw her talking to others, I would fight off panic that she would be sucked into a world of evil.

Since she was battling suicidal thoughts and hopelessness, she lived on a strange edge of inappropriate risk taking. This was a hard-to-describe reckless kind of behavior, like getting too close to the edge of a cliff when we were attempting a family vacation in the mountains or being too eager to be the one to climb up on a roof to retrieve a ball and then intentionally walking over to the edge. I often became afraid I might not be strong enough to stop her from being a danger to herself.

And what if her example would begin to rub off on the other children's behavior?

I remember coming to the end of many days raw and hurt and weary. I think I can understand why a hurt animal wants to curl up in a corner all by itself. It must be looking for the space of self-preservation—a place to shut out the danger around and nurse its hidden wounds. I found myself looking forward to bedtime as I cultivated my new habit of sleeping curled up on my side of the bed as far over to the edge as possible with the blankets pulled up all around me. I didn't want anyone to touch me or to come too near. Perhaps that's what David was experiencing when he wrote:

> Be merciful to me, LORD, for I am faint; O LORD, heal me, for my bones are in agony. My soul is in anguish. How long, O LORD, how long? ...I am worn out from groaning; all night long I flood my bed with weeping and drench my couch with tears. My eyes grow weak with sorrow; they fail because of all my foes.
>
> Psalm 6:2,3,6,7

I wondered how I as a mother of nine, helping to pastor a growing church, would be able to find a private space of my own to have a dark-night-of-the-soul crisis. I often fantasized about running away, but how, or where? Should I run away and take with me the child who was sick? Or, should I run away with everyone who wasn't sick but in danger of getting sick if Mom didn't get back to her senses? Should I just try to grab my husband's hand and run? Or, should I run all by myself and leave everyone to fend for themselves? If I did run away, where should I go? To an island? To a mountainside?

Or, to a new house with normal problems like sibling rivalry and potty training?

In reality, I couldn't even figure out how to imagine myself some relief. No doubt about it. I was stuck here to go through this dark night of the soul. The main key was that I had to stay out of the pit and find the power.

CHAPTER 5

The Pull of the Pit

The kind of pit I'm talking about is effectively identified in the book of Psalms when David said, "[God] lifted me out of the slimy *pit*, out of the mud and mire" (Ps. 40:2); and again, "Do not hide your face from me or I will be like those who go down to the *pit*" (Ps. 143:7). David was referring to the pit of eternal punishment called *hell*.[1] Notice in Psalm 143:7 that he didn't say he would be literally going to hell but that he was concerned he was going to experience the torture and torment of one going down to hell. That must be one nasty pit!

I am quite convinced my daughter Kalyn was living as one of those on their way to that kind of pit. She experienced a living hell pit on earth. It was horrible, treacherous, miserable, and tormenting. Perhaps you have a child living in one of those torturous pits. You may have lived in that kind of pit yourself, or maybe you are in a pit right now. If so, then you know the pit is not a place to wish on even your worst enemy!

A pit is deep, dark, and appears to have no way out (in the natural). The Hebrew lexicon describes it as a dungeon and a well.[2] Remember the well that Joseph's brothers threw him in before selling him into slavery? (Gen. 37:24.) John Gill portrays it in his commentary as dry but containing serpents and scorpions, which are two harmful vermin that symbolize "the devil, and his principalities and powers, and all his emissaries...their craft and cunning, and...their poisonous and hurtful nature and influence."[3] A hellish pit for sure! For a while I felt as if the devil had unleashed his "vermin" on me when I was being pulled into a pit with Kalyn during that crisis— truly a dark night of a mother's soul!

With the parent's soul weakened by its dark night attack, the enemy presses in harder with the pulling, tempting draw of the pit. He has subtle diabolical strategies (which we'll discuss in a moment,) but no matter what his personalized strategy was toward the child (abuse, sickness, rebellion, drugs, calamity, immorality, or something else), his plan is to pull the parents into his personally prepared "Parent Pit' as well. It's no surprise that the Parent Pit looks similar to the child's pit—anger, offense, bitterness, depression, alcohol, drugs, exhaustion, and so on—since the devil doesn't have any new pits or plans.

I call this pull of the pit a temptation to parents because some of the elements of the pit can seem temporarily comforting and inviting to a weary parent under attack in the dark night of the soul. Anger, bitterness, offense and revenge can feel strangely soothing to a violated or wounded heart. Emotional isolation from a spouse seems a lot easier than sharing the common pain. Depression allows the mind to shut down and temporarily give up the task of reasoning. Alcohol can help dull the pain. Drugs can provide a temporary escape. Even exhaustion and burn-out guarantee parents that someone else will have to take over life's management for a season and give them a break.

No doubt about it, temporary fixes can have some short-term gain. Because of this some might politely try to re-label the individual elements of the Parent Pit with more "politically correct" terms such as *coping mechanisms* or *involuntary responses*. In reality, the pit is still the pit and even a pit renamed will eventually produce torture, torment, and destruction—the enemy's ultimate strategy against all God built and created.

We know that God has a good plan and purpose for each human being He creates.

"You created my inmost being; you knit me together in my mother's womb. I praise you because I am fearfully and wonderfully made; your works are wonderful, I know that full well. My frame was not hidden from you when I was made in the secret place. When I was woven together in the depths of the earth, your eyes saw my unformed body. All the days ordained for me were written in your book before one of them came to be."

Psalm 139:13–16

"I know the *plans* I have for you," declares the
LORD, "*plans* to prosper you and not to harm you,
plans to give you hope and a future."

Jeremiah 29:11

Another verse in Jeremiah indicates that God's first
action in the life of a baby in the womb is to give that
child divine purpose and calling. (v. 1:5.) Then He places
that child in a family with its own purposes and callings.
Perhaps in our modernistic, war-torn culture we have
forgotten this simple fact. Of course, God doesn't force
any family (or individual) to follow Him and fulfill His
purpose and calling for them; in other words, He doesn't
intentionally place a child in an abusive family.

God created the family to be loving, caring, and
nurturing, but He also created each of us (that means
each parent too) with a free will to choose to follow Him
or reject Him: "I have set before you life and death, blessings and curses. Now choose life, so that you *and your
children* may live" (Deut. 30:19). The problem is some
parents don't "choose life"; they choose the world's
ways—and too often their children suffer for their wrong
choices. Still, since the beginning, the family has been
God's basic building block of human relationships, which
originated in the Garden of Eden. Later on God ordered
His chosen nation, Israel, by family groupings.

Because of the attack against the family in the last
two generations, twenty-first century Christians can
easily forget that God still wants to order and bless His
church through family groupings. He designs particular

giftings, callings, and plans for each family He creates through the covenant relationship of marriage. He designs the home to illustrate His love, His commitment, His order, and His creativity.

Our family's calling and ministry is unique to the Cherry family, but it is not somehow more important or better than your family's calling and ministry. That's the awesome reality of God's plan for the body of Christ. We are all made for His purpose and glory, with unique talents, giftings, and personalities. The point is that ultimately the enemy's attack over Kalyn's life became an attack over her parents, which became an attack over her whole family, which became an attack against anyone and everyone who God had preordained for her family to reach with the good news of Jesus Christ.

Since the enemy doesn't have any new plans up his sleeve, his basic battle strategy for families is to attack the weaker ones to get all in their sphere of influence pulled into the same pit. He saw our family as he may very well see yours—as a threat. So he searched for and found a weak place of vulnerability to launch his attack. In some families the weakest member at a particular season might be a parent. I know of several families who are in destruction today because the parent fell into the pit and the child followed after. The result of this plan is the same—the destruction of the whole family.

Our spiritual opponent designed his battle strategy to take control of as many individuals and families as possible and prevent them from advancing God's kingdom plans on the earth. I believe that one of the main tactics he uses to achieve this goal is to capitalize on our adult imagination limitations.

Strategies of Deception

Doug is an incredibly awesome father who takes very seriously the importance of connecting with the heart of each of our precious children. I remember a few years ago when he returned from a scheduled tennis outing with our five older children. As usual, the preschoolers were waiting for him at the door shouting, "Daddy, it's our turn now," and he responded, "Head downstairs, kids. We're going to play." He was obviously a man with a predetermined mission.

As the children scurried down the hallway, Doug enthusiastically explained to me that His plan was to have them assemble their favorite toy cars, trucks, houses, and people, and then together they would assemble a daddy-sized pretend village all over the basement floor. I forced myself to smile and replied supportively, "That sounds great!" but inwardly my heart sank. Over the years I had also tried many such play adventures and found that no matter what I did, I never seemed to play the game "right." Yet if any adult could achieve such a mission, it would be Daddy Doug.

For twenty minutes I could hear laughter and joy emerging from the basement as the clanging and banging of construction work proceeded. Then a strange period of silence followed all the noise, so I thought the casting of parts and pretend play had started. But the silence was soon interrupted by shouts of, "No, we can't do that!" and, "That's not how we play!" and

"Stop it!" Then Doug's voice rose above the clamor like a referee's whistle in the middle of a brawl. He tried to salvage the play by issuing new rules and directions, but the stubborn preschool imaginary characters wouldn't hear of it. All was no longer well in the basement village. Relationship-building was now replaced with relationship damage control as each child was sent howling to their rooms.

When Doug ascended the basement stairs, he looked more worn out than he had after his hour of hot tennis. I had to immediately repent for my feelings of glee. I was strangely comforted to know that I wasn't the only adult who had failed at pretend play!

What is it about the adult mind that bristles at imagination and is so logical and controlled that it rigidly fights to stay inside its lines of the rational seen world of existence? Perhaps the barriers keeping us from effectively entering into childish imaginary play are the same type of barriers keeping us from believing and perceiving the reality of the unseen spiritual realm all around us— even though the spiritual realm is a very real world charged with the activity of both God and His angelic ministering forces and the devil and his demonic tormenting forces. Then again, it's very possible that the devil himself has noted this adult human tendency and has found ways to capitalize on and exploit our perception weaknesses. Or maybe we adults do not often pause our daily life activities long enough to recognize and ponder his obvious activities in our midst.

Conceivably we are just so caught up in our reasoning and routines that we fail to understand Satan's mindset and strategies. After all, his tactics have been clearly recorded in over 2,000 years of world history. Unfortunately the masses of humanity are usually only able to perceive his activity as they look at it through the lens of the past. His strategies are never new, but they're always disguised within the cultural mindset and philosophies of the current day. We must know his strategies to keep our kids from falling into a deep, dark pit, and to avoid falling in ourselves. So let's see how he thinks.

Strategy 1: *Convince as many people as possible that Satan does not really exist.*

I fell for that one for years, as do many non-Christians and Christians alike. Studies by the Barna Research Group in 2009 indicate that only about 35 percent of polled *adult Christians* believed that Satan is a real entity.[4] So, what are we teaching our children? Since 70 percent of youth say there is no absolute moral truth, while 81 percent of our kids claim, "all truth is relative to the individual and his/her circumstances,"[5] in our kid's views, a real devil would only be true for me if I believed it were true. These statistics are evidence of a greater philosophical shift in this generation to what is called *postmodernism.* Josh McDowell, well-known speaker (especially to young people) and author, defines this as being the most common view of American teenagers today.

Before we jump to the conclusion that postmodernism with its doctrine of relativism is only a youth culture phenomenon, we must consider Barna's recent research examining changes in worldview among Christians over the past thirteen years.

> "Overall, the current research revealed that only 9% of all American adults have a biblical worldview.... One third of all adults (34%) believe that moral truth is absolute and unaffected by the circumstances. Slightly less than half of the born-again adults (46%) believe in absolute moral truth."[6]

The devil's first strategy appears to be working in many modern minds: No absolute truth plus no absolute reality plus no absolute existence of the spiritual realm equals no literal truth of God's Word, which equals no absolute existence of the devil.

Strategy 2: *Convince as many people as possible that there really isn't any spiritual realm battle going on, then keep them distracted by their own daily activities of life.*

Fill the airways with noise, activity, and clutter. Build a recreation-driven culture that is self-absorbed and busy. They won't even notice what's going on around them! Ron Luce calls this the culture machine that is attempting to hijack our whole household.

> "The culture machine is not just media, it is stuff— stuff to see, stuff to watch, stuff to go to, stuff to wear, stuff to give, stuff to drink, stuff that makes you pretty, stuff that makes you cool, stuff that makes you popular, stuff that makes you sexy, stuff that is fun to do, stuff that is adventurous, stuff that will live your life for you so you don't have to

go anywhere or do anything. Our lives are filled with <u>stuff</u>."[7]

Strategy 2 certainly seems to be effective!

Strategy 3: *Cause those who have discovered that Satan is truly real to be intimidated.*

Convince them that Satan is an overwhelmingly powerful and invincible foe so they will be afraid of his pressures and give up the idea of fighting. Some Christians act like the devil has more strength than God Himself!

Strategy 4: *After blinding or intimidating the masses, launch an attack against the weakest and most gullible members of society.*

This could be the young ones, or the injured, or the naïve—whoever he may devour. (1 Peter 5:8.)

Strategy 5: ***Use the attack of the weakest ones to distract and pull down the stronger ones.***

These five dreadful strategies are designed to destroy us and our families and stop the spread of God's kingdom on earth. Interestingly, they look remarkably similar to the wartime strategies described in my kids' history textbooks!

Get the Right Perception

Common elements of warfare in all cultures, people groups, and historical periods include deception, intimidation, surprise, strategies, battle lines, weaponry, victories, casualties, and defeats. I can understand if this coupling of military terminology with Christian concepts disturbs your peaceful image of the Christian faith. I emerged from my teen years with a liberal mindset and a pacifist lean, so this pairing would infuriate me. After all, I reasoned, isn't God all about love and peace? I even was one of those who joined the throngs to strike "Onward Christian Soldiers" from the hymnbook and "I'm in the Lord's Army" from Sunday school!

I think my confusion back then must have been the same confusion Jesus was countering in Luke 12:51 when He said, "Do you think I come to bring *peace* on earth? No, I tell you, but *division*." Though He knew He was the Prince of Peace (Isa. 9:6), He also knew that the very entrance of His light on the dark earthly scene would cause conflict and clashing and warfare.

The New Testament writer Paul understood this battle when he wrote, "Finally, be strong in the Lord and in His mighty power. Put on the full armor of God so that you can take your stand against the devil's schemes" (Eph. 6:10). He must have understood the battles the young pastor Timothy would face when he charged him to "fight the good fight of faith" (1Tim. 6:12). Paul certainly had firsthand experience with the force of the devil's weaponry when he was routinely beaten, persecuted, imprisoned, and shipwrecked; as he warned us, "Be self-controlled and alert. Your enemy the devil prowls around like a roaring lion looking for someone to devour. Resist him" (1 Peter 5:8–9).

So, after I came out of my own postmodern deception in 1991, I found myself proclaiming with other like-minded Christians that this life is "kind of like a war." Since then, I have come to understand that even this view was built upon a wrong perception. This life is not *like* a war, it *is* a war! Ron Luce spends chapters in his *Battle Cry* book describing the overwhelming agony of the increasing casualties of this actual war: a war waged against our own children and youth that is affecting both Christians and non-Christian homes alike, and is being executed by the prince of darkness to steal our children and weaken the kingdom of God's influence upon earth.

If you're still not sure the enemy's strategies are working, consider the following statistics: Between 69 and 94 percent of kids raised in Christian homes aren't following the Lord after graduating high school.[8] Only 4 percent of this current Millennial Generation (born 1984 or later) is projected to be Bible-based believers as adults. That is an alarming decline from the previous three generations' rates of Bible-based believers:

- ✗ Builders Generation (born 1927–1945): 65 percent
- ✗ Boomers Generation (born 1946–1964): 35 percent
- ✗ Busters Generation (born 1965–1983): 16 percent
- ✗ Bridgers Generation (or Millennials, born 1984 or later): 4 percent[9]

This is not a symbolic war, this is a real war! What a tragedy. Our unseen foe has waged a successful battle to annihilate the next generation's future while my generation has been asleep on our watch enjoying our comfortable luxuries and arguing over politically-correct language. We've silently allowed the media influences of television, movies, music, video games, and the Internet to reprogram our children's beliefs. We must wake up— our enemy is poised to take over our kids.

We shouldn't be surprised at the level of his onslaught against this next generation. From the beginning of human history, he's always been after the godly seed of a generation poised to usher in great revival and the advancement of God's kingdom. Remember when Pharaoh ordered all the baby boys to be killed at the time of the appearing of Moses (Ex. 1:22), and when Herod ordered all baby boys killed at the time of the appearing of the infant Jesus? (Matt. 2.)

Never before in history has the gospel had such potential for rapid advancement because we have the technological capabilities through satellite TV and the Internet to go into every nation with the gospel message. As we race to complete the great commission (Matt. 28:16–20) so that every language will have a witness of Jesus, the signs of the end of the age are all around us. (2 Tim. 3:1–9; Matt. 24.) The season of His second appearance is nearing and the devil surely is afraid of this next generation like no other. I believe this could be the generation to complete the charge of the great commission and take the good news of the gospel to all nations. Matthew 24:14 says that afterward Jesus will appear, the end will come, and the devil's days of reign on this earth will end.

To stop this from happening, the devil would have to unleash every weapon in his arsenal, starting by preventing as many as possible from ever even being born (Interestingly, statistics reveal that each year over 1 million American women choose to abort their babies).[10] He would have to work to unleash massive deception, steal the hearts of those born, and thus *destroy their potential* to be dangerous against the kingdom of darkness.

The weapons at the devil's disposal in this war against our children are numerous: violence, sexual perversions, pornography, cults, suicide, false religions, immoralities, media enculturation, eating disorders, AIDS, homosexuality, etc. While I'm convinced that he is carefully devising his best strategy and choosing his most effective weaponry against families, I'm not trying to make him seem more powerful than God. He isn't; Jesus defeated him on the cross 2,000 years ago and stripped him of his authority in the earth (Col. 2:15.) Still, the devil can mess with our lives and families if we're not aware of his *modus operandi*. So I've tried to reveal here the strategy of his plans to help you successfully win the war for your kids— and yourself.

His strategies may seem like a simple, effective, foolproof plan, but the devil isn't the only member of the unseen spiritual world who has a battle plan for families. I am absolutely sobered to realize that without God's miraculous grace and power operating on our behalf, we could have lost our daughter Kalyn and quite possibly our whole family and ministry. In the Cherry home, our heavenly Father's plan demolished the devil's best hit— and He can do the same for you!

Yet just being informed about the dangers of the pit won't keep us out of the pit. Just learning about the intricate details of the path to the pit won't be enough to keep us out of its snare. Knowing the devil's strategies won't be the sole factor in winning this war, either. We must learn to avoid *spirit failure* and employ *Spirit power*.

CHAPTER 6

Redeemed from Spirit Failure

Answer me quickly, O Lord: *my spirit fails.* Do not hide your face from me or I will be like those who go down to the pit.

PSALM 143:7

D avid was in the middle of a family crisis involving his son Absalom when he wrote this verse. Years earlier Absalom had killed his brother Amnon over a family tragedy and now he was trying to overthrow his own father, David, and make himself king. (2 Sam. 13,15.) David had fled for his life from his beloved son and in this verse David was crying out to God, claiming that his spirit failure was causing him to be drawn toward the torture of the pit. Reading that verse I so understand what David must have gone through. During our own family crisis, as I lived in the dark night of the soul, I could sense problems in my *soul*, but I also sensed that my own *spirit* was about to fail.

Remember, God designed and made us a three-part being—body, soul (mind, will, and emotions), and spirit. Our spirit is that part of us that will live on eternally in either heaven or hell after we die. When we submit ourselves to God and make Jesus the Lord of our life, God, through the person of Jesus and the power of the Holy Spirit, comes to dwell on the inside of us. (Gal. 2:20.) He makes our spirit new, cleansed, and whole. Jesus called that being "born again" (John 3:3,5) or "born...anew" (AMP), which enables us to hear His voice and yield to His power.

Since David lived in the Old Testament (and Old Covenant) era before Jesus came to earth, died on the cross, and rose again, the Holy Spirit could not dwell inside of David. (See John 14:16–17.) The Spirit could come upon people back then, but they weren't filled with the Spirit. (See 2 Chron. 20:14–15.) So David's spirit failure in Psalm 143 could be understandable because he was somewhat limited in his spirit power.

I, however, lived in the New Covenant era. I had Jesus dwelling in my heart. I was already born again and had the power of the Holy Spirit living inside of me. (Rom. 8:11.) I read my Bible and walked in God's ways. So how could I have come so dangerously close to a spirit failure that would have sent me to the pit with Kalyn?

As I encountered the dark night of the soul, my flesh was striving to dominate over my spirit. My emotions and fears and desires for escape from my struggles seemed to demand my focused attention. In my spirit, I truly did believe that God could miraculously pull my daughter out of the pit and keep me from going there with her, but a powerful battle raged in my mind as to whether I believed He would. The question became which one would rule over me, my soul or my spirit?

Two Bible translations of "my spirit fails" describe exactly where I was at that time: "my spirit is worn out" (GW), and "I'm at the end of my rope" (MSG). I was, as John Gill defined it in his commentary, "Ready to sink, swoon, and faint away, through the weight of the affliction."[1] Spirit failure was causing me to be pulled into the pit with Kalyn, *and I desperately needed an emergency supply of God's supernatural power*! Sadly, in the heat of the battle, it took me quite awhile to accurately diagnosis my problem. Yet, as always, God's Word held the answers to my questions.

I just love how God records in His Word the scenes of history for our spiritual instruction. Another place I find my own struggle depicted is Psalm 107. It's a remarkable portrayal of four different kinds of people who were under actual physical attack and close to spirit failure, yet were redeemed (brought back from destruction) from the hand of the enemy. We're going to look at each of them, for though this Psalm was penned some 3,000 years ago, it pictures twenty-first century humanity with incredible accuracy.

The Wanderers

Give thanks to the LORD, for he is good; his love endures forever. Let the redeemed of the LORD say this—those he redeemed from the hand of the foe, those he gathered from the lands, from east and west, from north and south. *Some wandered* in desert wastelands, finding no way to a city where they could settle. They were hungry and thirsty, and their lives ebbed away. Then they cried out to the LORD in their trouble, and he delivered them from their distress. He led them by a straight way to a city where they could settle. Let them give thanks to the LORD for his unfailing love and his wonderful deeds for men, for he satisfies the thirsty and fills the hungry with good things.

Psalm 107:1–9

The *wanderers* in modern times are the folks wandering through a spiritually dry land. They may be actively searching out spiritual answers to life's issues but have become confused by the current teachings of intellectualism, relativism, postmodernism, new ageism, Islam, Mormonism, Jehovah's Witness, and other false religions and philosophies. Or they may be just wandering around in desert wastelands uninterested in any of life's deeper questions.

Some of us spend years as wanderers before we find Jesus, who is the Way, the Truth, and the Life. (John 14:6.) But some of us spend a lot more years wandering about in a spiritual wilderness even *after* we meet Jesus, because we have not yet anchored our lives to His ways

97

and His Word. We are still trying to mix together our own ideas, the ideas of our culture, and His truth.

Wanderers find themselves in want. Though the promises of God are available to meet all their needs, wanderers grow hungry and thirsty and their lives ebb away. (Ps. 107:5.) They need answers and hope.

The Rebellious

Some sat in darkness and the deepest gloom, prisoners suffering in iron chains, for they had *rebelled* against the words of God and despised the counsel of the Most High. So he subjected them to bitter labor; they stumbled, and there was no one to help. Then they cried to the LORD in their trouble, and he saved them from their distress. He brought them out of darkness and the deepest gloom and broke away their chains. Let them give thanks to the LORD for his unfailing love and his wonderful deeds for men, for he breaks down gates of bronze and cuts through bars of iron.

Psalm 107:10–16

The *rebellious* have the same problem as the first created human beings, Adam and Eve. While living in their garden paradise enjoying a perfect relationship with God, Adam and Eve had only one easy restriction—just don't eat from a specific tree. (Gen. 2:16–17.) Pretty simple. Yet Adam and Eve believed they had a better idea than God Himself, and as they ate of the fruit of the forbidden tree, all of human history changed. (Gen. 3.)

Their rebellion against the words and counsel of God (Ps. 107:11) caused them to suffer "deepest gloom" and chains of suffering. (v. 10.)

That is the irony of those of us who live in some form of rebellion to God. What started out as a promise of personal liberty and freedom becomes our very chain of bondage. Some of us live in utter rebellion to all of God's Word and counsel. Some of us have just certain narrow areas of our lives in which we are stubbornly not submitted to God and His ways. We fool ourselves into believing God will ignore our sin. We count on His mercy while forgetting His holiness and His justice. We pretend that our sin is excusable and "different" from others, and all the while we are deceiving ourselves.

The Fools

Some became *fools* through their rebellious ways and suffered affliction because of their iniquities. They loathed all food and drew near the gates of death. Then they cried to the LORD in their trouble, and he saved them from their distress. He sent forth his word and healed them; he rescued them from the grave. Let them give thanks to the LORD for his unfailing love and his wonderful deeds for men. Let them sacrifice thank offerings and tell of his works with songs of joy.

Psalm 107:17–22

In the book of Proverbs, *foolishness* is portrayed as the opposite of godly wisdom. The writer of that book described *foolishness* as being bound up in the heart of every child. (Prov. 22:15.) I so can testify to the accuracy of that proverb! When I encounter one of my little ones stubbornly arguing that they didn't sneak candy while their mouth is covered in chocolate, I chuckle at their ridiculous foolishness. But when our heavenly Father sees us stubbornly refusing to follow His wisdom, I don't believe He is chuckling. He knows that our foolishness, because of our rebellious ways, will lead to suffering. (Ps. 107:17.) It's foolish to believe that anything other than His ways will ever truly prosper!

Sometimes our foolishness is the result of our current rebellion. Other times our foolishness is a result of an unrenewed mind that is still ignorant of God's ways and His Word. Ignorance grieves God's heart as He sees His children "destroyed from lack of knowledge" while their dusty Bible is sitting on the shelf. (Hos. 4:6.)

The Merchants
(Who Were Distressed and Discouraged)

Others went out on the sea in ships; they were *merchants* on the mighty waters. They saw the works of the LORD, his wonderful deeds in the deep. For he spoke and stirred up a tempest that lifted high the waves. They mounted up to the heavens and went down to the depths; in their peril their courage melted away. They reeled and staggered like drunken men; they were at their wits' end. Then they cried out to the LORD in their trouble, and he brought them out of their distress. He stilled the storm to a whisper; the waves of the sea were hushed. They were glad when it grew calm, and he guided them to their desired haven. Let them give thanks to the LORD for his unfailing love and his wonderful deeds for men. Let them exalt him in the assembly of the people and praise him in the council of the elders.

Psalm 107:23–32

What an interesting fourth category of suffering humanity. These people represent the ones who are busy doing their life work. They were mighty sea merchants. They knew the works of God and His wonderful, powerful deeds (v. 24), and they believed in His power. Yet when these merchants encountered a great and perilous storm (they were under enemy attack), "their courage melted away" (v. 26). They fell into the torment of fear and their faith gave out. Classic spirit failure! They lost their nerve and their way.

I can personally relate to this category so I believe I have a special understanding of these folks. They could be compared to us "Christian superstars"—doing the works of God, out in the deep revelations of His miracle power, but still unprepared to stand courageously through the mighty storm and resist the temptation of fear.

Verse 27 says that at one point these merchants "were at their wits' end" and so fearful they walked around as if they were drunk. One Bible commentary's remark on this is my favorite: "Those that have the Lord for their God have a present and powerful help...*so that when they are at their wits' end they are not at their faith's end.*[2]

The Pattern of Hope

All four of these groups in Psalm 107 were delivered from their distress. That's a great report. It's interesting, too, that if you look at how they got out of their troubles, you'll see the same scriptural pattern repeated in each of the four conditions.

✓ They cried out to the Lord in their trouble (vv. 6,13,19,28)

✓ The Lord delivered them out of their distress (vv. 6,13,19,28)

✓ They were exhorted to give thanks (vv. 8,15,21,31)

✓ They encountered God's unfailing love (vv. 8,15,21,31)

✓ They saw His wonderful deeds (acts of power) for men (vv. 8,15,21,31)

Here lies the good news of hope for us today: God wants to repeat the same pattern of hope in each one of our lives and families. What awesome news when trouble and darkness come upon us! He is just waiting for us to humble ourselves and cry out to Him. To *cry out to the Lord* means falling on our face and saying, "God, save me! I need You. You are my only hope. I cry out to You alone." So, when we place our lives in His hands, cry out in confession of our sins and failures, turn to Him, and seek Him and Him alone; then He is able to step into the midst of our pain and perform the miraculous. He will show us His awesome unfailing love and His wonderful acts of His power.

He will lead the *wanderer* by a straight and new way to a settled city.[3] He'll break the *rebellious* out of their chains and bring them out of their deepest gloom. He'll heal the *foolish* from their afflictions and rescue them from the grave. He'll still the storm of the discouraged and distressed (the *merchants*), and guide them to their desired haven.

Perhaps you are like me and can see yourself some-where in Psalm 107. Maybe like me, you have person-ally experienced all four of these human states at one time or another. As I think back over my life, I realize that if I had encountered some type of dark night of a mother's soul in 1985, I would have found myself in group 2—the *rebellious* state. If I had encountered an attack on Kalyn's life in 1989, I would have found myself in group 1—the *wandering* state. If I had encoun-tered the dark night of a mother's soul with my third child Lucas in 1994, I very well could have been in group 3—the *foolishness* state—for though by that time I had been radically changed by the power of God, He was frequently revealing to me my own foolishness based on my ignorance of His ways, my unrenewed mind, and my past areas of rebellion to His Word.

I believe that in 2002 the state of group 4 best described me when I was in the dark night of my soul over Kalyn. Doug and I were much like the *merchants* in verse 22. Our spiritual ship had finally been launched out onto the deep waters of pastoring and pioneering a church, and we were seeing the mighty works of the Lord and "His wonderful deeds in the deep" (v. 24). Yet when a great storm arose, my courage melted away, fear overtook me, and I became distressed and discouraged.

Rescued from Spirit Failure

I remember October 23, 2002—several days into our parenting crisis. We were in Tulsa at the Leadership Conference trying to hold our family together in front of hundreds of observing eyes. Kalyn was growing more difficult and defiant by the hour as Doug and I were growing more confused and embarrassed. We found ourselves having a "family meeting" in the back rooms at the Victory Bible Institute.

That meeting with Kalyn proved to be our most horrifying one of all. With very cold, calm, deceived eyes she looked straight at us and announced that our relationship with her was over and that our family was never going to be the same again. She said that we had ruined her life by the way we had raised her. She declared that she was "never coming back," and warned us that we were destined to lose our other kids as well due to our parenting flaws.

I looked at this shell of my daughter sitting before me and was convinced that it was not really her speaking to us anymore. The daughter I knew would never say such horrible things. As our storm now raged into a tempest, whatever spiritual strength I was previously operating with seemed to just run right out of my legs. I found myself weeping and wailing in horror. I even remember literally reeling and staggering around the room in my distress (just like Psalm 107:27 describes). I said things that contributed to the darkness and trauma of that night. I remember turning to Doug and saying, "That's it. We've got to quit the ministry. I've heard of this before. People stepping out boldly into new works of ministry and then the devil attacks them hard and they end up losing their family. I can't do this anymore. I'm not going to lose my family!" I wept and shouted.

There sat Doug weeping and watching in horror as his daughter seemed totally taken over by darkness and his wife seemed dangerously close to panic and complete spirit failure, with a newborn and a toddler crying at her side.

In that awful, unforgettable moment, Doug spoke what would prove to be defining words for our battle ahead, "We cannot and will not negotiate with the devil. He is a liar and a terrorist. If we try to quit the ministry right now, he will take our church and our family too. I know that if we'll trust Him, God will deliver us all out of this mess."

I'd like to be able to report that right then and there all my fear stopped and all my faith in God arose. It didn't, but Doug's faith-filled declaration dropped an anchor in the midst of our storm and set the stage for a remarkable increase in our spiritual power. God's grace flooded to our rescue—but I still had to find the path out.

If you were suddenly hit with a dark night experience in your life, could you avoid spirit failure? Or would you find yourself in one or more of the four spiritual conditions described in Psalm 107? I encourage you to pray the prayer below for whichever spiritual condition you may be in right now, and expect God to rescue you and help you to find your own path out!

If you are living your life as a *wanderer*, it's time to come to Jesus. You can give Him your life right now by praying this simple prayer:

Dear Father, I've spent my life as a wanderer trying this and that to find meaning and purpose. I've trusted in the world's systems and in myself. I ask You, Lord, to forgive me of my sinful ways. I've broken Your Holy Laws. I've tried to be the Lord of my own life. Sometimes I've even pretended like You don't even exist. I ask You to forgive me, Lord. I turn from trusting my life to anything or anyone but You. I turn away from all darkness. Jesus, I believe in You. I believe You died for my sins and You rose again on the third day. Please come into my life and be my Lord, be my boss. I choose to obey You and serve You. I ask You, Lord, to heal my wounded heart. Teach me Your ways. My answer to You in advance is yes, Father! I will obey. Thank You, Jesus, for living Your life in me. I love You. In Jesus' name. Amen.

If you are living in *rebellion*, you can repent of going your own way by praying:

Dear Father, I can see my own life is so similar to Adam and Eve's. I've not wanted to obey Your ways. I've thought I knew best. That's pride and rebellion, Lord, and I know Your Word says that pride goes before a fall and rebellion is as the sin of witchcraft.[4] *I repent of all rebellion, especially of the following acts* [insert your own personal sins]. *I renounce them as sin and I now turn to Your ways of obedience. Whatever Your Word says is true, Lord, and I choose to obey Your every instruction. I know You have my best interests at heart. I ask for Your wisdom, guidance, and strength. Thank You, Lord. I love You. In Jesus' name. Amen.*

Perhaps you are walking in *foolishness*. Then it's time to learn God's ways of wisdom for you and your family. Just pray this prayer:

Dear Father, as I look over my life I am convicted of my own foolishness. Your Word in Proverbs 22:15 says that I was born with foolishness in my heart, and Father, I can see that much foolishness is still there. Lord, I know Your Word is full of wisdom. Forgive me for not taking the effort to store up Your Word in my heart. Forgive me for my stubborn, rebellious ways. I ask You to bring forth wisdom into my life as You promised in James 1:5. I thank You for pouring Your wisdom upon my family and me. I ask that You will watch over Your promises to us and cause us to begin to build our lives on You and Your Word. I love You, Lord. In Jesus' name, amen.

Are you like the *merchant* traveling on the high seas but in danger of discouragement? It's time to truly trust the Lord.

Dear Father, I've chosen to trust You as my Savior. I love You, Jesus. I've known of Your mighty deeds and power in my life in the past. But here I am Lord, fearful and doubting that You really will take care of all my storms today. Please forgive me for my fear and lack of faith. I humbly ask You to restore my courage again. Cause me to desire Your Word like never before. Cause me to fix my eyes upon You. I take my place of rest with You under the shadow of Your wings. I trust You, Lord, and I will walk on in Your power. I love You! Amen.

Don't ever risk your life or your family's to *spirit failure* that leads to the pit! Our heavenly Father is waiting for us to cry out to Him and take the next step. With the devil pressing his strategies against our homes, it would be foolish to not prepare them to stand against his onslaughts. This is the day to start preparing and find the power to win!

(If you have prayed any of these prayers, we would love to hear from you and help you with further resources. Go to Kalynssecret.com)

CHAPTER 7

Hooked Up to the Power

*T*he two-hour drive home from the St. Louis Airport felt like an eternity. My heart was crushed and hemorrhaging, yet somehow I was able to smile and carry on light-hearted conversation while replaying in my mind the tapes of the VBI meltdown scene. With Kalyn safely asleep in the back of the van, I counted the minutes until I could deposit the whole family back in our 6-bedroom split-level. All I could think about was having privacy in our seven-acre home, with its surrounding fields and woods nearby.

Cherry family homecomings are never quiet, and when the van pulled in the driveway, everyone went running in their own direction—some to check on pets, others to unpack new treasures from Grandma and Granddad's house. I grabbed the baby and attempted to hide myself for a few minutes in the master bedroom. My escape was short-lived as my expertise at unpacking was required. After 45 minutes of controlled mayhem, one of the younger children asked, "Where's Kalyn? We can't find her anyplace."

"I'm sure she's here somewhere," I said with a forced smile. My heart speeded up as I hurriedly searched the whole house and yard, then headed outside to find Doug. I calmly but firmly told him that Kalyn was missing, knowing that his mind would be flooded with the same thoughts as mine had been. We had both witnessed Kalyn's horrible speech to us in Tulsa just 48 hours prior, and now she was gone.

Could she have called the man, arranged a meeting, and left with him? Could she have walked down the road to hitchhike or found a way to the bus or train station? Is she systematically working on an escape plan or just randomly expressing her desperate emotions? My first wave of questions was troubling, but my second wave was horrifying. Is Doug's hunting shotgun still in its case? Does she know how to load it? Are there any knives missing from the kitchen? Do we own any dangerous prescription drugs?

Doug must have drawn the same conclusions, for when Nathan arrived on the scene moments later, I heard Doug quietly ask him to go get both of their hunting guns and hide them deep within the attic rafters. Nathan, wide-eyed, quietly hurried to obey.

I thought my legs were going to crumple as I fell into Doug's arms, crying. A quiet strength came over him as he gently said, "I was praying about this situation the whole way home on the plane. I believe the Lord spoke to my heart three things. First, He promised me that He is going to bring her out of this. But, secondly" he quickly added, "He also warned me that things were going to get a lot worse before they get better. I just didn't realize how quickly the word He spoke to me *would come to pass. We've got to do the third thing He said to do— trust Him and believe."*

There it was again...an anchor in the midst of the storm.

After several hours of Doug and Nathan alternating drives down the road with hikes in the woods, while I stayed at home by the phone, we were about to call someone somewhere about Kalyn when Nathan spotted something red wandering slowly across a distant field. As we sat in the living room watching, the red sweatshirt quietly drew closer to the house and slipped into our basement back door. Doug was the first to greet her, but all she could do was walk through the door and fall in a crumpled heap to the floor, quietly weeping. Gone (for a few days) was the angry, defiant teenager and any words of explanation. Now we simply rushed to put blankets around our cold, broken little girl...

We might be able to make it a whole day before we rediscover our need, but usually it's only a matter of moments or hours after awakening that our heart feels the pang of a lonely yearning, or our mind discovers the alarm of an empty questioning. It seems that our world is constantly flooded with the reminders of the limits and vulnerabilities of our human condition. Some try to silence the reminders by pretending they don't exist. Yet let the morning news of another tsunami disaster, a senseless school shooting, or a friend's baby born with an untreatable heart defect penetrate our day, and we will be cognizant, if only for a moment, of the frail state of our human lot.

Ever since Adam and Eve walked out of their garden paradise we've had to compensate for our loss of power. That isn't what God intended for His awesome creation called *man*. (Gen. 1:26.) Originally, God bestowed upon Adam and Eve, the first parents, the power needed to complete their jobs of being fruitful, multiplying, and ruling over the things of the earth. (v. 22.) After all, they were created in the very image of God Himself, who is *omnipotent* or "all powerful."[1] (v. 26.) Yet contained within the power that God had given to *man* was also God's incredible gift of the power of free choice. Unfortunately, the first man and woman didn't handle that gift well. With their willful disobedience to God, they gave their power away to the devil. Ever since then people, in our natural state, have been held subject to the one whom Jesus called the god of this world. (2 Cor. 4:4 KJV.)

When I think of the traumatic event with Adam and Eve, I imagine our heavenly Father with a broken heart and tear-stained face as He had to send them out of their paradise home—broken, wounded, sorrowful, and powerless. (They must have been very reluctant to leave, as Genesis 3:24 says that God had to literally drive them out.) I believe that as He watched their weak and confused forms walk away from His presence, He could already see within them the muted silhouette of two grieving parents standing on a driveway thousands of years later, also broken, wounded, sorrowful, powerless, and in desperate need of His supernatural, miracle-working power.

Yet the garden scene departure in Genesis 3 was not the end of *man's* story. God didn't leave us helpless and hopeless. At the very moment of Adam and Eve's mess up and their cutoff from God's power supply, He began to work His *redeeming* (reclaiming of power) plan—the one He had devised "before the creation of the world" (1 Peter 1:20).

The Answer to Every Problem

God first revealed His restoration plan in the same chapter of the Bible where it is written about Adam and Eve's sin: He would send His Son, Jesus, to restore what had been stolen by the devil.

I will put enmity between you and the woman, and between your seed and her Seed; He shall bruise your head, and you shall bruise His heel.

Genesis 3:15 NKJV

Jesus, the woman's Seed God spoke of here, came to Earth to take back the *power* that Adam and Eve had given away to the devil when they disobeyed God. Jesus accomplished this through dying "to put away sin by the sacrifice of himself, and to destroy him who had the power of death, that is, the devil. Thus [Jesus] bruises his head—destroys his power and lordship over mankind, turning them from the power of Satan unto God."[2] So through Jesus our "power hook up" was restored. That's why Paul calls Jesus the second Adam and explains His *power-restoring provision* this way:

> For if, by the trespass of the one man, death reigned through that one man, how much more will those who receive God's abundant provision of grace and of the gift of righteousness reign in life through the one man, Jesus Christ. Consequently, just as the result of one trespass was condemnation for all men, so also the result of one act of righteousness was justification that brings life for all men. For just as through the disobedience of the one man the many were made sinners, so also through the obedience of the one man the many will be made righteous.
>
> Romans 5:17–19

The devil, in his dialogues with Jesus in the wilderness, tried to tempt Jesus to take back the dominion and authority of this world by bowing down and serving him since he (the devil) was the one possessing that authority at the time. (Luke 4:5–8.) He failed because Jesus understood that the Father's plan for restoration would never include bowing a knee to Satan. He knew that God's plan would destroy Satan's dominion and return that dominion to mankind where it originated—and Jesus knew that the plan could only be completed by the shedding of His blood on the cross.

As Jesus was walking through His earthly ministry, He demonstrated His dominion and power, which got Him into trouble with the chief priests and teachers of the law. Jesus was speaking to the people as One who had authority, not as the scribes whose teaching lacked that kind of authority and the power of God to touch people's souls.[3] For example, in Capernaum, while He was teaching in the synagogue, He cast out a demon from a man. Everyone was so amazed at His teaching and miracle power "that they debated among themselves, saying, 'What is this? A new teaching with authority! He commands even the unclean spirits, and they obey Him'" (Mark 1:22, 27 NASB).

That story is repeated in Matthew and Luke, as all three writers use the Greek word *exousia*. (Matt. 7:29; Luke 4:36.) *Exousia* refers to force, superhuman mastery, and delegated influence, which reflect authority.[4] This Greek word was important to Doug and me because it contained the answer to our problem in our driveway that October day. In fact, *exousia* holds the answer for every problem anyone is facing now or in the future.

In the New Testament, *exousia* is translated "power" 69 times, "authority" 29 times, and "right" 2 times.[5] No doubt the people of Jesus' time clearly understood this strong word. So when Jesus was described as having *exousia*, naturally He upset the religious leaders. His teaching had *authority*. His miracles demonstrated His *power*. And He was clearly establishing His *rightful place* of Lordship. Yet, His mission was not just one of demonstration—it was one of restoration.

Jesus gave His authority back to His children. At one point He "summoned His twelve disciples and gave *them* authority [*exousia*] over unclean spirits, to cast them out, and to heal every kind of disease and every kind of

sickness" (Matt. 10:1 NASB). In speaking to the 72 followers He sent out in Luke 10:19, Jesus said, "Behold, I have
given you *authority* [exousia] to tread on serpents and scorpions, and over all the power of the enemy, and nothing
shall injure you" (NASB). And at His closing exhortation to
His disciples in Matthew 28:18 He said, "All authority
[*exousia*] in heaven and on earth has been given to me.
Therefore go and make disciples of all nations."

Clearly Jesus had the *exousia,* and He transferred the
exousia to His true followers. God said of Jesus through
John, "To all who received [Jesus], to those who believed
in His name, He gave the right [power, authority—
exousia] to become children of God" (1:12). This verse
reveals who has the privilege of *exousia* over the spiritual
forces of darkness: To have *exousia* we must be a true
child of God—we must have repented of our sins,
proclaimed Jesus as our personal Lord and Savior, and
been born into His kingdom by the new birth (see John
3:3; Acts 2:21). So, not everyone who calls themselves a
Christian has *exousia.* Neither can we just hang out at a
church and have *exousia* (just as we can't hang out in a
garage and claim we're a car).

Luke recorded this truth in operation when the sons
of Sceva tried to imitate Paul's authority over demons:

> The evil spirit answered them, "Jesus I know,
> and I know about Paul, but who are you?" Then the
> man who had the evil spirit jumped on them and
> overpowered them all. He gave them such a beating
> that they ran out of the house naked and bleeding.
>
> Acts 19:15,16

To have victory over the kingdom of darkness operating against our homes, we must have authority or *exousia* through our new covenant relationship with Jesus.

When Doug and I were staring darkness in the face during Kalyn's crisis, it was imperative that we had *exousia*, and that we knew how to operate in it. Our prayer of agreement was critical. (Matt. 18:19–20.) Our posture of faith in God's Word was vital. Our ability to say no to Satan's activity in our midst was essential. These came through a scriptural understanding of our authority in Christ. Believers who have not been taught the truth of their authority will let their hands fall limp to their sides in the day of battle and easily be convinced to not even fight. Because of our *exousia* we can stand up and proclaim, "In Jesus' name, I command every force of darkness to leave my home."

Believers who take up their authority are believers who will win their battles!

Explosive Power Hook-up

While *exousia* generally is translated as "power" in the sense of authority, another essential Greek word meaning "power" is *dunamis*. Jesus said in Acts 1:8 that we would receive *dunamis* (power) when the Holy Spirit comes on us. To better understand this second power hook up, let's look at some examples.

The earth was formless and void. The *Spirit of God* hovered over "the face of the deep [the waters]." And

God spoke, "'Let there be light,' and there was light" (Gen. 1:2–3).

A young girl named Mary was visited by an angel of God and told that she would bear the Messiah. Then, the *Holy Spirit* came upon her, and the power (*dunamis*) of the Most High overshadowed her, and she conceived the Son of God. (Luke 1:31–35.)

Peter failed Jesus miserably. In Jesus' most desperate hour, Peter slept instead of prayed, denied instead of defended, and hid instead of watched. But Jesus, when He rose from the dead, told Peter and the other disciples to go to Jerusalem and wait for the "power [*dunamis*] from on high" (Luke 24:49). As they waited in the Upper Room, suddenly a sound like a blowing wind filled the whole house. Tongues of fire rested on them and they were *filled with the Holy Spirit* and began to speak in other tongues. That same day Peter boldly faced his accusers, preached his first gospel message, and 3,000 people were saved. (Acts 2.)

A group of men were gathered to pray over their sin-filled city of Los Angeles in 1904. A small group of sincere believers in Jesus, they earnestly sought God's deliverance power from the darkness that had gripped the town when suddenly the Holy Spirit's presence fell over their meeting. People began to prophesy and speak in tongues as those did in Acts 2. Thus, the great Azusa Street Revival was birthed with thousands of salvations locally and a revival fire that continues to spread worldwide even to this day.

In each instance, the Holy Spirit *dunamis* happened. It is the word from which we get our English word *dynamite*.[6] *Dunamis* is used 120 times in the New Testament to mean "a mighty working miracle power."[7] Did Doug and I ever need some *dunamis*—explosive power—when we were standing in our driveway that day in October, 2002!

Jesus Himself operated in this Holy Spirit power anointing when He healed the sick, walked on water, and cast out unclean spirits. It was written of Jesus at the start of His ministry that He returned to Galilee, from His wilderness experience, in the *dunamis* power of the Spirit, and news about Jesus spread through all the surrounding district. (Luke 4:14.) Acts 10:38 says, "You know of Jesus of Nazareth, how God anointed Him with the Holy Spirit and with *power* [*dunamis*], and how He went about doing good, and healing all who were oppressed by the devil, for God was with Him" (NASB).

That same *dunamis* is available to all believers by being filled with the Spirit. I am a living testimony that His *dunamis* has not passed away. He is working His power through those who humble themselves and believe. When the Holy Spirit shows up, the miracle-working power of God comes! And His *dunamis* did show up for Doug and me.

The Force of Love

As I stood in the driveway staring disaster in the face, I knew something about my *exousia* in Jesus Christ and about my need for the *dunamis* of the Holy Spirit. Yet I was months away from my discovery of the precious power of the Father—His *agape*. Oh, if you had asked me that day about the awesome *strength* of the Father, I could have given you a nice biblical-sounding answer. After all, what Sunday school child hasn't heard about the Father's powerful *agape love* for them? But little did I know that this third prong of my power hookup would prove to be my most critical revelation.

God the Father brings the power of *agape* to the Trinity. I believe it is what the Bible describes as "the river of the water of life" (Rev. 22:1), and in recent times has been sung about as the "reckless, raging fury that they call the love of God."[8] To separate the force of the Father's healing love from His nature is impossible. As the apostle John wrote (under the inspiration of the Holy Spirit), "God is love [agape[9]]" (1 John 4:16).

Love (agape) can best be understood as a spiritual force—a force of the kingdom of light that drives back the forces of darkness and gives the ultimate sacrifice. The apostle Paul helped us understand the power of the Father's love in this passage:

> Love [agape[10]] is patient, love is kind. It does not envy, it does not boast, it is not proud. It is not rude, it is not self-seeking, it is not easily angered, it keeps no record of wrongs. Love does not delight in evil but rejoices with the truth. It always protects, always trusts, always hopes, always perseveres. *Love never fails.*
>
> 1 Corinthians 13: 4–8

Who could ever forget the demonstration of that agape power in action in the parable of the prodigal son? (Luke 15:11–32.) When the younger son was given his inheritance early by his father, the son dishonored his father by foolishly spending his fortune on wild living and sinful lusts. But the father stood by patiently until the son came to his senses, repented of his foolish ways, and returned to his father's house. Even when the son ran from him, the father never left his post of love! When his son returned, he lavished his love and forgiveness upon his wayward child. The father's agape love never failed. I also found that our heavenly Father's agape love never fails.

I'll never forget that horrible day several months into our family struggle. I was exhausted. Kalyn's irritable, rebellious behavior had the whole household in an uproar. For weeks I could sense the very frightening state of my own mother's heart. The stress, anger, and sorrow were just too much. Now even my memories of peaceful days spent with the precious little girl whom I had nursed, rocked, and laughed with were beginning to fail me. I couldn't conjure any more sweet warm feelings of love and devotion for her. Maybe it was one horrendous verbal encounter too many. I just remember running to my room, falling on my bed, weeping and crying out, "Lord, help me! I don't feel feelings of love anymore for my own daughter." I was terrified by my emotions. After all, no decent mother could ever lose her feelings of love for her own precious child!

Lying there in my awful, miserable state, I could feel my heavenly Father holding me gently in His arms (not physically, but in a spiritual sense). Then He spoke His clear, calm words of comfort to my heart. "You are going to witness something you've never really understood or needed before. You will see the power of My love operating through you. And My love never fails. It can't. It is not based on anything but Me."

So began my new journey of faith: Faith in a Father's love that could flow through me to my daughter. Faith in a love that wasn't based on anyone's cuteness or performance or feelings. Instead, I was to discover the powerful, miracle-working spiritual force called love *that's based solely on a written promise by a covenant-keeping God—and the truth of His promise that His agape never fails.*

A Trickle or a Full Supply?

Even with our postmodern mindset many people seem to accept the concept of supernatural power. I haven't heard in recent days any debate of the question so popular in my youth: "Is God dead?" I do hear a lot of debate on the how's, where's, and who's of supernatural power. A walk through grocery store check-out lanes reveals our fascination for the supernatural, with tabloid headlines like "Psychics Predict in 20xx," "Stars Discover New Evidence for Reincarnation Experience," and so on.

It appears we were all created with what is often termed a "God-shaped hole." Out of that hole will eventually emerge our cry for help. Some will call upon Allah, or their higher power, or their own human reason and intellect. Yet as Moses discovered at the Red Sea with the Egyptian army close behind; as Joshua discovered when his small army marched around the massive walls of the fortified city of Jericho; as Gideon discovered when his army of 300 faced an army of thousands—*our God is the Most High*! His power will always defeat the devil, the one Paul called "the god of this world."

Our God is the same God of the Old Testament patriarchs and of the New Testament disciples. He's the same God of the early church Fathers and even our American Founding Fathers. He is Almighty God. El Shaddai! The God who is more than enough. The Creator of the ends of the earth. He is the One who calls Himself the Alpha and the Omega—the Beginning and the End. (Rev 1:8.) He is timeless, ancient, eternal, unchanging, without blemish or defect, and completely holy. He is the only Way, Truth, and Life. (John 14:6.) He has offered Himself, His love, His relationship, and His provision of grace and power to all people through all ages, all nationalities, and all times. Nevertheless, this doesn't mean mankind has or will find it. To those who understand His ways, who respond to His incredible offer of a covenant relationship, who obey His principles, and who can believe His incredible mercies, He will make His supernatural power available.

My choice that day in 2002 was the same as every other person's choice. I could choose *spirit failure* or *spirit power*. Quite honestly, I had experienced my share of spirit failures in the past, so I knew what Doug spoke in the driveway was absolutely right. We, in our natural selves, were not going to be able to muster the power needed to save our daughter. We were going to have to *completely* plug in to God and His supernatural spirit power. Limited earthly 110 and 220 voltage of self-help was simply not going to do it. We needed the whole power supply of the Father, Son, and Holy Spirit!

Is your life linked up to the full power supply offered to us by God? Or are you currently settling for a mere trickle of His power? Are you confidently able to look ahead to any challenge that the enemy of your life and family could throw on your path and know that his best plans could not stand against God's promised plans?

When Jesus spoke to the religious group of Sadducees in Matthew 22:29, He sharply rebuked them on two important counts: "You are in error because you do not know [1] the scriptures or [2] the *power of God.*" Many of us are in the same error. We have failed to know and build our faith and our lives on the promises and provisions of God's holy Word, and to appropriate every aspect of His power into our daily living. We might have survived our own error before—but the times and seasons have changed. God is calling to His people to awaken and live lives of courage and victory. We need not live in confusion and terror, in dread of the day of evil. We can live in confidence and boldness, trusting in an almighty God who has and always will deliver His people.

I encourage you to abandon all fear of the devil's schemes and boldly take up your *exousia* in Christ. Study God's Word for yourself. Know who you are *in Christ.*

Build up your faith in God's provision of authority and stop being intimidated by the devil's lies. And if you are ready to see some of that explosive, miracle-working *dunamis* power of the Holy Spirit operating in your life and family, then yield to all the Holy Spirit desires for you. Perhaps you need to stop worrying about what others will think of you. The fact is, you might begin to look different than the world's crowd—but shouldn't we, as God's representatives, look a little bit different than the current lost and dying culture? Banish all fear of man and go after all God's power supply for you and your family.

If you are ready to see your life turned upside down by the reckless, raging fury of God's love, then let Him into your dry and wounded heart first. When you begin to allow Him to heal you, His overflow of *agape* love will begin to flow through you to your spouse, your family and other loved ones, and to all those in your sphere of influence who are hurting in this lost and dying generation. I know that God is ready to give us the fullness of His power—He's promised to in His Word. We just need to plug in!

CHAPTER 8

The Secret Power Gifts

God's power is available to everyone who becomes born again and filled with the Holy Spirit. Yet no teaching on the power of God would be complete without covering what I call the *secret power gifts*. They can only be accessed by those who are willing to pay the price, and the cost can be high—time, reputation, effort, and even personal comfort, to name a few—a price that many of us aren't willing to pay. It's like placing undesirable-looking Christmas gifts under the Christmas tree. They are wrapped with plain brown paper and string, and hanging from each present is a price tag displaying a high cost. Anyone who chooses one of those gifts has to pay the price on the tag. The cost would deter most adults from picking them.

The cost of the secret power gifts can be just as undesirable (*and* challenging), but that didn't deter Doug and me from picking them because we learned in our home that these power gifts from God were not only helpful, but essential. So in this chapter I'm going to show you what we learned and why these gifts truly are worth the price, starting with perhaps the most costly of all.

The Power Gift of Brokenness

A few years ago I remember singing a worship song that talked about brokenness and how brokenness is what we long for, need, and what God wants for us. I sang that song in church like everyone else there, with heartfelt passion. But when true brokenness hit my life during Kalyn's crisis, my flesh didn't think it was what I longed for or needed!

To some people *brokenness* implies things falling apart, crushed, and weak. (I don't know about you, but I hate weakness!) Others think of a horse—broken of his own will and completely yielded to the will of his master. Both of these images apply to the spiritual concept of brokenness. While not pleasant, my own brokenness yielded good fruit: My pride was broken. My trust in my own perfection, my own reputation, was broken. My trust in my own self-power was broken. My independent, self-sufficient ways were broken. In the midst of my broken mess, I was humbled; yet in my humility, I found my heavenly Father.

Every time I had to call a professional counselor, retell our story, and ask for help, I was humbled. Every time I had to report to someone that we had failed to install Internet controls on our computer or check the kids' emails, I was humbled. When we had to call fellow pastors and ask for prayer, I was humbled. When my most admired spiritual mentor advised Doug and me to fight this spiritual battle by asking the Lord to search our own hearts for sin and pride, I was humbled. When we had to answer police and lawyer questions, I was humbled.

In the midst of my brokenness, I was reminded of the story of David, when he was broken down by the convictions of his adulterous sin with Bathsheba. (2 Sam. 12:24.) He wrote in Psalm 51:17, "The sacrifices of God are a broken spirit; a broken and contrite heart, O God, you will not despise." But, my mind objected, David's condition was different. He had clearly brought on his own destruction by obvious, blatant, willful sins. Why should I be humbled when I didn't willfully sin? I didn't cause the perversion or the damage to my child. "This wasn't fair!" I cried. I was a good mom doing good things for my child. I was a righteous woman living a clean and holy life. Before your mind attempts to do what my mind did—defend itself and reject the concept of brokenness as "unfair"—let me explain about the "fair" situation in which Doug and I found ourselves.

Every parent needs a fair amount of wisdom to lead their children—but we needed parenting wisdom beyond average measure. Every parent needs a fair amount of love for their children—but we needed parental love that ran deeper than the average measure. Every parent needs a fair amount of faith to believe for a successful parenting outcome—but we needed faith beyond the average reasonable store. In short, we needed more than our "fair" share of everything! We needed God's share of miracle power. And God knew that. So He led Doug and me into a more than fair state of brokenness.

Only God knew the secret condition of our own human hearts. In fact, He knew our conditions better than we knew them ourselves. He knew that without a breaking of the hard places of our hearts the river of His power would never be able to flow to our rescue. It would simply be deflected off as rainwater deflects off of a dry, parched ground. He knew that when we stood up to the voice of our accuser, the devil, we would attempt to defend ourselves and shout back at him, saying, "I am totally innocent of any wrongdoing," and then suddenly our own hearts would condemn us! What person can ever say that he or she is totally without any sinful motive, any sinful action, or any neglectful failure? How could we ever believe, think, or say we were perfect parents completely without errors? So God allowed us an unpleasant but necessary journey into our own brokenness (or weakness).

I reluctantly had to face the fact that my personal weaknesses of pride, selfishness, and stubbornness had hurt my daughter and our relationship together. I had sometimes allowed my sin to erect walls in our communication. Oh, I didn't want to think about it, because it seemed so overwhelmingly painful to admit. Did my sin cause her destruction? No. Was I the one to blame for all of her great pain? No. Still, my sin was unmistakably intertwined in the whole painful mess.

Reluctantly, I had to face the fact that I had been inattentive to the abuse warning signs she was displaying. (For warning signs of sexual abuse, see Tool 2.) Partly, I was inattentive because I had acted in ignorance; partly I had ignored those warning signs because of my own pride and fear of man. That sin didn't cause Kalyn to be attacked and hurt, but it had to be factored in to the situation. Ignoring my sin didn't make it go away; justifying my sin didn't silence the devil's accusations of blame. Saying that my failures were only 5 or 10 or 20 percent of the problem didn't wipe away their significance.

My only real hope was to allow God's conviction full place in my heart. Only when I was truly broken because of *my* sin—not the sin of others—could I really cry out in repentance to the Lord and allow Him to cleanse me with His blood and then replace my weakness with His strength. Suddenly, I understood what God meant when He told Paul, "My grace is sufficient for you *for my power is made perfect in weakness*" (2 Cor. 12:9). Paul wrote in the next line, "Therefore I will boast all the more gladly about my weaknesses, so that Christ's power may rest on me. That is why, for Christ's sake, I delight in weaknesses, in insults, in hardships, in persecutions, in difficulties. *For when I am weak, then I am strong*" (vv. 9–10).

Amazingly the Lord's strength began to arise in me as I opened His gift of brokenness. Instead of cowering in my bed under the pain of guilt and condemnation, I could face my enemy square in the eye and say, "You're right, devil. I did have some failure mixed in here. But my sin is under the blood of Jesus. You can't accuse me with it anymore. For where I was weak, my God has promised to be strong." As I learned to resist the devil through God's power of brokenness, he began to flee from me. My mind became clear.

Then I could hear my heavenly Father's voice of wisdom and instruction in my heart. Brokenness, instead of being my dreaded enemy, had become my best friend.

The Power Gift of Truth

The debate over the concept of truth is nothing new. While our postmodern philosophies may be pressuring us to give up on the concept of absolute truth, Adam and Eve knew that same pressure in the Garden of Eden when the serpent said to them, "Did God *really* say, 'You must not eat from any tree in the garden'?" (Gen. 3:1). Pilate at Jesus' trial knew that same struggle when he asked the profound question, "What is truth?" and then proceeded to pass sentence on the Son of God. (John 18:38; 19:1–16.)

God the Father knows of our human struggle with issues of truth. That's why Jesus, in revelation of the Father's heart, very clearly stated, "I am the way, *the truth,* and the life. No one comes to the Father except through me" (John 14:6 NKJV). That's why He had the psalmist declare, "All your words are *true;* all your righteous laws are eternal" (Ps. 119:160). That's why He had Paul in his instruction to the young pastor Timothy command him to correctly handle the word of *truth.* (2 Tim. 2:15.)

Jesus is the Word made flesh. (John 1:14.) He told us how and why to build our lives upon the Rock[1] (which represents the Lord and His Word):

> Therefore everyone who *hears these words* of mine and *puts them into practice* is like a wise man

who built his house on the rock. The rain came down, the streams rose, and the winds blew and beat against that house; yet it did not fall, because it had its foundation on the rock.

Matthew 7:24,25

Hearing the truth, believing the truth, and then *acting* on the truth keeps our "houses" (our souls,[2] our lives, our families) standing against the storms.

When Doug and I faced our greatest parenting challenges with Kalyn, we needed the power of truth. We needed, more than at any other time in our lives, to bolt ourselves down to the Rock of truth. We held on to every promise written in His book as if it were written personally to our family.

God would remind us that Psalm 112:1–2 says, "Blessed is the man who fears the LORD, who finds great delight in his commands. His *children will be mighty in the land*; the generation of the upright *will be blessed*." So we had to remind ourselves that since His Word is truth, Kalyn would indeed be mighty in the land and all other circumstances (such as Kalyn being trapped miserably in her own bed) were temporary.

Likewise, when God would remind us that all our children (including Kalyn) had been taught of the Lord and "great [is] your children's peace" (Isa. 54:13), we had to remind ourselves that God's Word is always the final verdict no matter what temporary torment she was experiencing. When God would remind us that He sent forth His Word and healed all our diseases (Ps. 107:20), we had to remind ourselves that depression would not be able to stay in Kalyn's body. When we saw strange demonic activity happening in our home, we had to remind ourselves of the truth that we have been given "authority to tread on [snakes] and scorpions, and over all the power of the enemy, and nothing will injure [us]" (Luke 10:19 NASB).

Basically, it became a choice of what we would believe. Would we believe the horrible report coming from our daughter's own mouth and our own imaginations or would we believe God's Word?

Never have I experienced such temptation to give in and compromise on the issue of truth. Never have I felt such pressure to make gentle choices, even if just in my own mind, to "soften the truth." But I knew better than that. I knew that it was only the truth that would set us free! (John 8:32.)

When Kalyn would dress in ways that were inappropriately seductive and alluring, how I wanted to ignore what I saw. Oh, how I wanted to avoid the conflict and change my standard of "truth." How I was tempted to soften my preaching on sin and change my parenting style. When I could clearly see that my daughter was rejecting God and His ways and turning toward the ways of darkness and of the world, how my mind wanted to reduce the problem down to a more comfortable and manageable size. How I wanted to rename the rebellion and hardheartedness as simply a temporary developmental stage she would grow out of. But I knew better than to give in.

I knew that my secret place of power was to embrace all the truth of my situation as God saw it. All of God's Word is truth. All of God's promises are truth. All of my problems were also true. And ultimately God's truth and His Word over my situation would win out over my problems!

We can't afford to be ignorant of the pressures of our modern age. It is not easy in this generation to continue to stay in the truth. The media assaults our minds. The philosophies of humanism and atheism are taught in our schools. Deception is all around us. Yet Jesus warned us that in the last days, "many false prophets [false proclaimers of truth] will appear and *deceive many people*" (Matt. 24:11). I frequently remind myself of one of my favorite sayings: "It wouldn't be deception if it wasn't deceiving." In other words, if you are truly deceived, you won't know it! Until, of course, the light of God's Word and the power of the Holy Spirit open your blind eyes. So, we *must* have the truth of God's Word as the light to our path and the lamp to our feet. (Ps. 119:105.) It is the plumb line by which to judge every decision and direction that comes our way.

Have you answered the question, "What is truth?" Are you prepared to stand on the truth of God in the face of persecution and trial? Are you prepared to lead your family confidently and boldly in the power of His truth? We can't wait another day to bolt down our lives and families to the Rock that can't be moved no matter how strong the storm. We can't wait to beseech the Father to search our own hearts for any pockets of deception or false foundation. Our very lives depend on our accurate handling of God's truth.

The Power Gift of Forgiveness

I had never seen Doug so angry before. After 22 years of marriage, I had certainly seen him have multiple opportunities to stay enraged, but he never did. He had matured to a point of almost sainthood in my book in regards to forgiving others and releasing offenses. People would rise up and do something ugly to us, and he would calmly say, "I refuse to stay angry. Lisa, just forgive them and let them go. No offense. No bitterness." Then he would turn around and bless the people who had mistreated him. I knew he was right, but I sure had to work hard to catch up to him.

I naturally just assumed that Doug had done the same thing with the man who had abused Kalyn. I assumed his angry outburst in our bedroom on October 19 was dealt with and over. So when I heard him confess to Kalyn after months of her crazy state of denial about this man that forgiving the perpetrator was still one of the greatest battles of his life, I was both relieved to know that I wasn't the only one still struggling to forgive, but alarmed to know that we had not yet won the battle of forgiveness.

The secret power released through forgiveness is actually most graphically illustrated in reverse, for while forgiveness opens the pipeline to God's healing power over our lives, unforgiveness completely blocks that healing flow. Jesus taught this principle quite clearly in the parable of the unforgiving, unmerciful servant. (Matt. 18:21–35.) In this parable a certain servant was forgiven a great debt by his master, but that same servant went out and refused to forgive a smaller debt owed him by his fellow servant. When the master heard about how the wicked servant treated his fellow servant, he reinstated the wicked servant's first debt and had him thrown into prison.

Jesus clearly was teaching us the danger of unforgiveness—if we don't forgive others, neither can our heavenly Father forgive us. (See Mark 11:25.) We clearly don't want to get caught on the outside of God's forgiveness and mercy!

I had a large challenge ahead of me. How would I be able to forgive the man, forgive Kalyn, and also forgive myself? I found that it was only through the power of God, only through a quality faith-filled decision of my will, only by daily thanking the Lord for removing my stubborn heart of unforgiveness and giving me a soft heart of mercy, and only by recognizing that there was a horrible consequence of failing to forgive: a bitter root would grow in me! By that root God promised that many would be defiled—in other words, the bitterness could spread to others. (Heb.12:15.) Satan's tempting web of revengeful spite would ultimately lead to the forces of death and destruction inside of me and my relationships.

Of course, this doesn't mean that forgiveness is only achieved when forgetting takes over. If I had to wait to forgive until I was able to forget, I could have a lifetime of waiting! Forgiveness is not a matter of forgetting, but it is a matter of releasing. According to Christian author and speaker Gary Smalley:

"Releasing your offender can drain several ounces of resentment at once, and it usually involves learning how to forgive. The original definition of *forgiveness* actually means that you untie or release someone. As long as you remain bitter and unforgiving, you're tied to that person with emotional knots. So being untied involves a conscience and deliberate release of the offender through an act of forgiveness.... An important though difficult part of releasing someone is giving up the expectation that the person will eventually see the error of his or her ways and take the initiative to make things right with you."[3]

Forgiveness doesn't mean ignoring all discipline and punishments for wrong doings. When a child sins, it is the parent's job to release him or her completely from the offense even while applying proper discipline to cause the child to learn from that sinful action.

In our case with Kalyn, reporting the crime to our authorities and then cooperating with their criminal proceedings was necessary to ensure proper discipline of an unrepentant heart and protection of other children. But it was imperative for us to forgive and release this man even as we faced him in a courtroom setting. God cares about his healing and restoration, just as much as He cares about ours—and because God cares, I am called to care, too. I do not believe this man intentionally set out to hurt our daughter. I do believe his own struggle with sin pulled him into a deception and darkness that he can only be released from through his own heartfelt confession and repentance. I pray for his complete recovery and restoration, and that God will heal his wounds and bless his life. Anything less from me would be wrong.

Most parents will face opportunities to hold on to unforgiveness as we raise our children. The offense may come at the hands of a stranger, or perhaps it will come through the hands of someone we love. It could come through the actions of our own child—or even ourselves. However it tries to come, purpose in your heart in advance that you will not hold on to offenses. John Bevere, a well-known author and evangelist, teaches that offense is the bait of Satan sent to destroy.[4] We have been given a great measure of forgiveness by our heavenly Father, and He expects us to offer that forgiveness to others. (See Luke 12:48.) That is His secret power at work in us!

When Doug and I left our church in Oklahoma to begin pastoring in Illinois, we left with some excellent words of advice from our pastor: "If you don't get bitter, you'll make it in ministry." I think the same advice is good for parents (and everyone else regarding their lives). If we don't get bitter, we will make it through parenting!

Brokenness, *truthfulness*, and *forgiveness* are blessings from God, not hindrances. When we walk in these godly principles, all the power of the Father, Son, and Holy Spirit can be released into our lives and the lives of our children. So go ahead—open those gifts and get strengthened and blessed!

CHAPTER 9

The Parent's Place
of Authority

*A*s I awoke one hot, muggy Southern Illinois day in July of 2003, I proceeded through what had become my morning routine—one not enjoyable, but designed to rescue my day from certain disaster. It seemed that no matter how I distracted myself as I awakened, the thoughts of the previous days' stresses and traumas would hit my mind like a runaway freight train. Whatever the cause of my pessimistic anxiety—nighttime dreams that were so miserably disturbing that my brain awoke already fatigued, or emotions that were worn and raw—I knew my only ray of hope was to grab my Bible, begin praying, and wrestle my own thoughts into God's order of peace. My kids needed a mama who could face the day with confidence and strength.

As I began my prayer time that day, I knew I had so much to be thankful to God for. Kalyn really was quite a bit better. She had been on antidepressant medication for six months and was no longer clinging to her bed. Her thought processes were much more reasonable. In fact, she had only a couple weeks before broken completely free of her confusing denial state about the abuse while on a lunch outing with Doug.

When he asked her if she was ready to talk about what had happened with the man (which we had asked her on a regular basis for months), she suddenly said, "Yes, I'm ready to talk." Then right there in the car amidst tears and sobs, the true story finally poured out of her mouth. That was also the day when she said she knew that what this man did was wrong, dangerous, and illegal. She wanted to tell that same story to the police. I was shocked when Doug called me on his cell phone to say that they were on their way to the sheriff's department.

As I hung up my phone, I wondered why she suddenly chose that day to share the details of her story. Did she really want help dealing with her troubled world of reality or was it for a less noble reason? Perhaps she was simply tired of living in a 16-year-old limbo state without her driver's license. Her driver's education had been completed for months, but she knew we would not be giving her permission for a license until we could sense she was ready to receive help for her months of trauma and erratic behavior.

Doug and I had struggled over that decision. We hated to disappoint her on her sixteenth birthday or to become the "bad guys" again in her mind and withhold the car; she had been through so much trauma and disappointment. But we couldn't send her out into the world driving a car unsupervised when she was still living in an inaccurate world of denial. How could we trust that her emotional state would allow her to make mature choices? There was just no way we could hand *her those car keys and take those risks. We had to believe that one day she would thank us for our firm, clear stand.*

This day, I was thanking God that we had received phase one of the reward of our tough discipline stand—her vow of silence was now broken!

Filing a Police Report

The police station visit went well. The officer was so kind as he gently questioned and probed her story. He did a great job of explaining to her that she had been a victim of a long "grooming process,"—a tricky, subtle, psychological manipulation that had caused her to freely participate with the perpetrator's instructions while hating it and keeping her vow of silence at the same time. The officer commended her for coming forward to the authorities to tell the truth.

Doug was able to reveal to the police the Internet dialogues Nathan had accidentally found stored on our home computer several months prior. The dialogues contained instructions from the man to Kalyn to "keep our secret," dating way back to when she was fourteen years old. It really seemed to help Kalyn to have someone other than her parents diagnose that she had been a victim of a crime.

Doug and I had talked with the deputies months prior, and they had advised us that there was no hurry to file our police report. In fact, they recommended that we wait until Kalyn was able emotionally to come out of her silence and make the statement voluntarily. Doug had spent many hours praying about whether a police report was really necessary for us to do.

Would we just needlessly increase our family's pain if we reported the abuse? Shouldn't we just practice "kindness" and all try to "forgive and forget" what had happened? But what about our responsibility to other families and churches who could be affected by this man's unethical behavior?

As Doug listened for the Lord's direction in this matter, he became convinced it was necessary for us to make that report to our authorities. As law-abiding citizens, reporting illegal activity positioned our family on the side of truth and justice. And truth would, as we were standing on it and believing, set all of us free—including Kalyn and the perpetrator. What the authorities did with this truth would then be up to them.

When she arrived home from the police station, she looked like a different child. Though her behavior was still not our normal Kalyn, she looked as if some invisible thousand pound weight had been lifted off of her shoulders. And for the first time in months she expressed some angry feelings toward the correct target—the abuser— instead of toward herself or us. We thanked God for this breakthrough, yet we knew we had much more ground to take back. It was still too painful for her to tell the officer about the exact details of some of the phone dialogues. More recovery time was needed.

Turning Point in the Battle

As I finished my prayer time that day in July, I was somewhat relieved. My whole family was at least operating in the same world of reality! But while Kalyn was finally able to label the abuse as abuse, she was still very confused as to how *the abuse happened. To her, our "oppressive parenting" had driven her to need to be rescued by this man who had become her confidant and advisor. While the same household rules had been normal and understandable to her in the past, now under the influence of full-blown teen rebellion, they seemed tight, unfair, and ridiculous to her. So daily she was suspicious and hostile toward any of them like chores and bedtimes and rules of etiquette.*

Everyday life was still very much a battle. I found myself trying really hard to make as few parental directions and commands to her as possible because I hated the bristling, edgy, surly responses she made to even my simplest requests like picking up her coat or cleaning her dishes. My very motherly presence seemed to even evoke hostility. It was a miserable way to live. So on that day in July, my nerves were in the new normal state: raw and preset for battle. I worked hard to cover it all with a smile, but inwardly my spiritual weapons were always in my hands, and my mind was always alert for trouble.

Kalyn had been pushing the line with me all day, challenging my directions and comments. We had entertained a group of her teenage friends as they played basketball and swam in the pool throughout the afternoon. Finally, evening was approaching, and I was about ready to call it a day. Little did I know my greatest parenting demand for the day was just beginning.

I didn't recognize the car that entered our driveway that afternoon, but a couple of the car's passengers I knew I had seen before. A sick feeling immediately hit the pit of my stomach. My mind began racing as my pulse began rising. Immediate warning alarms were screaming in my head. One look yielded a quick diagnosis. These new kids were clearly trouble, and it appeared they wanted to escort Kalyn into trouble with them.

I watched out the window as Kalyn began chatting animatedly with the driver and the other passengers. I saw her head toss back in a playful, flirtatious laugh as they gestured her toward the car. My hand instinctively reached for the phone. Thankfully Doug answered quickly. "Come home immediately," I said emphatically, "It looks like Kalyn's going to try to leave our house with some kids who appear to be trouble!"

I knew that he could be home in less than five minutes as his office was just about a mile down the road, but I wasn't sure I had five minutes. I began to pray and cry out to the Lord for help. I commanded the forces of darkness off of my property. I prayed for the protection of the blood of Jesus to descend upon my daughter and my home. Then I glanced out the window. I knew instinctively this could be a major turning point in our battle for Kalyn—either toward life or toward destruction.

Soon I watched Kalyn walk through the front door. "Mom," she said rather flippantly, "these kids want me to go with them for a while. I'm going, okay?"

Right then and there I knew what the enemy was up to. Our parental authority and leadership would be again directly challenged, and my role was already cast in this scene. At that moment I hated my part to play for I knew there would be a new season of persecution unleashed by my decision. But what else could I possibly do? My voice was surprisingly low and steady. "No, Kalyn, honey, you can't go," I calmly responded.

Almost immediately, as those words left my mouth, Doug's car pulled into the driveway and blocked our visiting car. I saw *him head toward the driver's window as I watched the stormy anger rise in my daughter's face.*

"You never let me do anything!" she yelled as she stormed back out the door. I wasn't sure what was going to happen next in this pivotal moment. Would Kalyn yield to my command or defy me and return to the car and drive away?

I was amazed when almost immediately the car started its engine. Kalyn's quick response to the driver and Doug's presence in the driveway were transforming the scene very quickly. The car was leaving, Kalyn was crying and running to her room, and I stood at the window horrified, crying, and relieved. That day's battle with evil was won.

I'm sure that on that day in July we weren't the first or only parents of a teenager to endure a challenge or threat to their parental authority and leadership. That same kind of horrible, torturous parenting scene is replayed in front yards all over America every week. I know that because I hear about those scenes from parents at the soccer fields, the shopping malls, and in the church hallways where we gather together.

Sometimes the stories conclude as ours did—as a narrow escape from teenage disaster. More often, though, the story concludes with a sad, anxious parental report of, "She wouldn't listen, and she went out anyway. Now we have even bigger problems." Or sometimes the story concludes with an even more common response. A long, deep parental sigh is accompanied by a negative headshake and a resigned conclusion, "Well, she's sixteen. What could I say to her? I had to let her go and make her own decisions." Immediately when I hear these words, I have to bite my tongue before I offer an unsolicited retort of, "You could try just saying *no!*"

Usually I can perceive that if I were to offer my opinion, my advice would not only be considered socially inappropriate or rude, but also seem outdated, insensitive, and perhaps even dangerous. I certainly can understand why. Most modern parents know about the "modern experts" concluding that autonomous decision-making and social independence are healthy needs and unquestionable rights of all modern teenagers. Nearly all the popular magazines draw that conclusion. It certainly seems to be the norm we see in the majority of TV sitcoms, movies, and the Hollywood scene.

With such horrible difficulties and pains overtaking our current generation of teenagers, some important questions need to be answered: Who are these "experts"? Who are these people who are helping us raise our kids, and are we sure that their theories are correct? Are teenage trauma and rebellion the developmental "norm" that we should, as parents, prepare ourselves to expect? Is it possible that we, as parents, have been deceived into adopting a cultural mindset, which is actually damaging our ability to successfully lead our kids through teenage temptations to maturity? Is it possible that our own passive form of parental leadership is opening the doors to disaster? Are we unfairly expecting our children to make decisions that they are ill-equipped to handle?

It seems that in our efforts to be "modern," we actually have become naïve, foolish, and backward, particularly when we wonder if we're really "normal" as parents if something deep inside of us wants to rise up and take charge of our wayward teens. Perhaps we can understand this inner parental conflict by noting what many of us like to view on television.

Hold Up the Shield

It's interesting to note the fascination in recent years with one cable television network's reruns of the previous generation's family-friendly shows like *The Andy Griffith Show*, *Leave It to Beaver*, and *Father Knows Best*. Is it possible that these shows are touching on some sort of God-given desire placed inside each of us to surround ourselves with more normal and healthy family role models? Perhaps while we laugh at Ward and June Cleaver[1] and claim that their strong parental leadership and no-nonsense home order will damage our modern, free-spirited prodigies, inwardly we know better.

Something written on our hearts can actually recognize the truth—proper parental leadership, authority, and rules mixed with obvious loving parental devotion to children actually bring peace, order, stability, and freedom to the next generation. So we hunger for what we really need: parenting role models who more closely line up with God's original design for families.

The pressures on our kids nowadays are part of a larger cultural phenomenon. Parents are now entering a second reaping of the rebellious seeds sown in America and other parts of the world during the 1960's and '70's. Those years are commonly known as the era when Grandma's well-proven morals and values were tested and found too restrictive. It was the era when "the establishment" was tested, and the rules were changed to become "less oppressive." In this current generational crop, however, the fruit of those seeds is not bearing well! While our kids' generation is wandering around in a humanistic pastureland of no moral absolutes, evolving truths, and free love values, our generation must recognize that we're the ones who opened the gate to their pasture. We bought into the lies and the deceptions of a cultural shift that is threatening to collapse our modern families from the inside out through a family system of anarchy.

The shifts and changes in the modern belief systems are well documented and staggering. We saw earlier that this new philosophical belief system has been given a name—*postmodernism*. It's been defined as "a theory that involves a *radical reappraisal* of modern assumptions about culture, identity, history, or language."[2] Yet while *postmodernism* is a descriptive word often thrown around in the popular press, its exact definition is not well understood. Nevertheless, its logical result is what we see today: a whole generation of teens who are being conditioned by popular culture to believe that "truth is not true for them *until they choose to believe it.*"[3]

Josh McDowell says of postmodernism:

"Trying to define and truly understand postmodernism can be a lot like standing in an appliance store trying to watch three or four television shows at once. It defies definition because it is extremely complex, often contradictory, and constantly changing.

"In fact, it's fitting that the very term *postmodernism* describes this school of thought by *what it's not*. In other words, postmodernism is the philosophy that succeeded and, to some degree, supplanted modernism, a way of thinking that has itself challenged the Christian worldview for centuries. Whereas modernism rejected religion and superstition in favor of science and reason, postmodernism repudiates any appeal to reality or truth.

"So, while postmodernism is tough to pin down, it is possible to summarize its most common beliefs:

✗ Truth does not exist in any objective sense.

✗ Instead of 'discovering' truth in a 'metanarrative'—which is a story (such as the Bible) or ideology (such as Marxism) that presents a unified way of looking at philosophy, religion, art, and science—postmodernism rejects any overarching explanation of what constitutes truth and reality.

✗ Truth—whether in science, education, or religion—is created by a specific culture or community and is 'true' only in and for that culture.

✗ Individual persons are the product of their cultures. That is, we are not essentially unique individuals created in the image of God; our identities are defined by our culture (African-American, European, Eastern, Western, urban, rural, etc.).

✗ All thinking is a 'social construct.' In other words, what you and I regard as 'truths' are simply arbitrary 'beliefs we have been conditioned to accept by our society, just as others have been conditioned to accept a completely different set of beliefs.'

✗ Any system or statement that claims to be objectively true or unfavorably judges the values, beliefs, lifestyle, and truth claims of another culture is a power play, an effort by one culture to dominate other cultures."[4]

It's obvious that this postmodern understanding of truth erodes any foundation for parental authority—and now those same beliefs are apparently coming from many parents, as only 22 percent of *adults* claim to believe in absolute moral truth.[5] That way of thinking is having a serious, negative effect on our children.

It's possible and I believe probable that: as we have shifted our cultural beliefs, we have dropped our shield of moral protection over our own children; our own false beliefs of relativistic thought (*truth is only true if I accept it for me*), pluralistic values (*there is more than one truth*), and evolving truths (*truth is changing*) have opened the door to a family government system of anarchy—each parent, each child constructing his or her own truth and ruling his or her own self.

In this postmodern society, wouldn't "parental commands" by definition be reduced to a concept of "parental suggestions"? It would seem that the unfortunate pressures of broken homes, multiple parents, and blended sibling groups have caused us to fold under the pressures of the seeming confusion. Have we become so afraid of the rampant problems of parent bashing, parent blaming, and teenage rebellion that we have simply abdicated our proper roles of leadership and left our poor children—and ourselves—wondering, "Who's in charge of this family anyway?"

Who *Is* in Charge?

I remember when Nathan and Kalyn were little, and I was eagerly combing the modern parenting literature of the 1980s for the most up-to-date solutions to my parenting questions. I was insecure and fearful that I might not parent them correctly or I might bring damage to their young lives. I felt pressured by the modern literature to give them as much autonomy and decision-making room as I could, lest they be limited in their cognitive or social development. And while I secretly held disdain for those mothers who couldn't figure out how to appropriately give their young children free choice in the cereal aisle of a supermarket and also avoid a loud ruckus, I was convinced that my sweet innocent little Nathan could handle the cereal decision with only gentle mothering suggestions by me. For the most part, he generally did—but then came baby #2, Kalyn.

Kalyn was so much more like her mother—more opinionated and vocal. After a few tries down the cereal aisle with my daughter, I immediately began to suspect that my mothering-by-gentle-suggestions leadership style might not make it through the next 18 years with her! From the onset of those first baby steps, she seemed to be asking that normal childhood question that Nathan rarely asked, "Mom, who's in charge here anyway?" Oh, she never formed that question with her mouth. It was more in the look of the eyes and the frustrating temper tantrums. I found myself ill-equipped to answer her question. Confusion, frustration, and motherhood stress were the result. Thank God, He didn't leave me in such a bewildered state.

From the moment my eyes were opened to the truth and accuracy of God's Word in 1991, I discovered a new hope in my parenting as well—but also a new challenge. I began to understand how much I did not yet understand. I started to see how my modern philosophies about many things including my marriage and my parenting were directly impacting my children. I realized that my very foundational beliefs were actually blocking God's blessings in my family's life. So day by day He began to teach me from His Word about His principles of authority and leadership. Surprisingly, what He taught looked nothing like what I was experiencing in the world around me.

Prior to 1991, my feminist driven point of view (which was the norm of everyone I knew at that time) had caused me to carefully discount from my Bible all the scriptures relating to the concept of "headship" or "authority" or that nasty *s* word— "submission." After all, this was twentieth century America, the land of the free and the home of the equal. *In our home, we'll have two equal heads, thank you. That's the enlightened, modern, educated way!*

It was not a problem for me to work this belief with my Christian faith for I had learned to label all the scriptures related to such issues as the husband is the head of the household as being culturally irrelevant and incompatible to modern thought. (This method of biblical interpretation is called *higher criticism.* Its rise in the church closely parallels the rise of postmodernist thought.) That is why it was such a shock to Doug on that day in 1991 when I approached him with the news that I wanted to submit to his leadership as the head of our household. *Head of our household?* he must of thought. *There's no such thing. We've always had two heads!* He was left totally speechless as I tried to explain to him that God had convicted me of my antiauthority and rebellious attitudes toward His ways that were so deeply ingrained in my postmodern mindset.

I remember quoting Ephesians 5:22–24 for Doug, which says:

> Wives, submit to your husbands as to the Lord. For the husband is the head of the wife as Christ is the head of the church, his body, of

which he is the Savior. Now as the church submits to Christ, so also wives should submit to their husbands in everything.

God was doing a big work in my heart. In fact, He was beginning to restructure my whole worldview by first restructuring my core philosophies.

Looking back I'm still not exactly sure how God orchestrated that spiritual breakthrough in our lives because Doug was deeply influenced by a feminist worldview as well. But on that day in 1991 something amazing happened in our home. We both received the grace of God to simply embrace the simple truth of His Word. I was to submit to Doug as the head of our home. He was to love me as Christ loved the church. Our children were to honor and obey us as the God-ordained leaders of their lives.

Suddenly a new peace and a new order settled into our marriage and our home. Joy replaced our striving with each other, and God's sweet presence flowed through our household decisions. No longer were we two heads butting against each other. As we no longer strived to maintain our own boundaries and rights, God began to reveal to us the equally important but awesomely different roles of the husband and wife. I was able to communicate freely my insights and desires in our household decisions while Doug was able to bear the weight of the tough headship role. Truly, God was teaching us His ways.

CHAPTER 10

God's School of Obedience

From the time of our birth, we've each been enrolled in what I call God's school of authority. I didn't understand that when I held my first baby (Nathan) in my arms like I did when I held my tenth baby (Josiah). Obedience is God's way, so this lifelong obedience-to-authority training course begins by learning to obey our parents and eventually obeying other authority figures (teachers, police, and so on). What I like to describe as the "kindergarten" years of that course happen in toddlerhood when we learn to respond correctly to our first "No, don't touch" command. What a critical season of our life childhood is! Those who can pass God's school of obedience to natural human authorities will be able to mature in life. Those who fail His obedience school as children are destined for great pain.

We see that all around us—from teen rebellion (against authority) that has led to school shootings and the installation of metal detectors to confiscate weapons from students, to more than two million Americans living behind bars, denied their freedom because they refused to submit to proper authority. God implemented submission and obedience to proper authority for our own good. His ultimate goal, however, was not only that we comply with the commands of our parents, teachers, and civil authorities[1] but that we learn loyal lifelong obedience to the voice of our wise and just heavenly Father.

How can we obey an authority we have never seen (God) on the basis of the printed Word (the Bible) if we have never learned to obey authorities we have seen (parents, teachers, police, and others) on the basis of their spoken word (or spoken commands)?

Since Adam and Eve failed their first authority test in the garden, obedience hasn't come naturally to mankind. Willfulness and rebellion come naturally. So most of us reach our adult years (even if we have given our lives to Jesus at a young age) with some ground to take back in our ability to quickly and totally obey God and His Word.

The issue of authority is an important key in rescuing this generation from disaster. Has your household passed successfully through God's school of authority, or are you currently failing out of His program as Doug and I were all those years ago? God's system is not some optional plan we can opt out of if it doesn't suit our fancy. It is *truth,* and truth doesn't change.

Whether you are a parent or are raising children in another capacity (legal guardian or grandparent, for instance), you can check out your own progress in this area by answering these questions: If you have younger children, can you give them a direction and be relatively sure they will obey that direction the first time without complaining or delaying? If you have teenagers, does your firm but loving no change their direction, or does your no seem like only a suggestion blowing in the wind? If you are a wife, are you submitted to your husband's leadership? If you are a husband, are you obeying God's Word completely, and sacrificially loving your wife?

Thank God my no to Kalyn that day in the driveway, though not graciously received by an angry teenager, did succeed in stopping her behavior. Thank God Doug and I had enough restraint over her during those dangerous days that we could keep her safe when she was not emotionally or mentally capable of defending herself. What if she had not been trained in obedience at an earlier age? What if she had not been taught to fear God and honor authority? Would she have walked out of the house that day and entered a whole new realm of teenage trouble? Only God knows for sure.

What if Doug and I had not received God's correction and had not begun to build a proper foundation for authority in our personal lives and our home? Would we have had the foundation of faith to take God's promises and, like the Roman Centurion, believe Him for our miracle? Perhaps you remember how the Roman Centurion was a Gentile, a person of a non-Jewish nation and faith. Yet when he faced an impossible situation with his servant, he believed that Jesus could give him a miracle:

A centurion came to [Jesus], asking for help. "Lord," he said, "my servant lies at home paralyzed and in terrible suffering." Jesus said to him, "I will go and heal him." The centurion replied, "Lord, I do not deserve to have you come under my roof. But just say the word, and my servant will be healed. For I myself am a man *under authority*, with soldiers under me. I tell this one, 'Go,' and he goes; and that one, 'Come,' and he comes. I say to my servant, 'Do this,' and he does it." When Jesus heard this, he was astonished and said to those following him, "I tell you the truth, I have not found anyone in Israel with such great faith."…Then Jesus said to the centurion, "Go! It will be done *just as you believed it would.*" And his servant was healed at that very hour.

Matthew 8:5–10,13

We see in verse 9 that the centurion understood authority and obedience. He was a soldier who was subject to the commands of others with higher rank; he also had authority over men under him who were subject to obey his commands. He believed in who Jesus is and that just as his commands were obeyed, how much more sickness and disease (and everything else) would obey Jesus. You may be thinking, *But I didn't start off on the right foot of obedience to proper authorities and to God.* Let me encourage you that it is never too late to start passing God's school of obedience.

God's school is not like any other school system. He allows us to retake our tests until we pass! I'm living proof of that. Perhaps you are a married woman and you feel that you have failed to honor your husband's authority in your home. You can repent and begin immediately. That is important because if we are planting seeds of rebellion toward our own husbands, we will undoubtedly be reaping on those seeds in the hearts of our own children. Yet we can stop this negative, spiritual process right now by repenting to the Lord. In time, our children will begin to follow our example. That is also true for men. If you are a husband and father who hasn't taken your proper place of authority as the head of the household and you haven't led your family in Christlike love to the truth of God's Word and His ways, you too can repent and begin a new path today.

The good news is that if you as a parent, grandparent, or legal guardian have temporarily lost one of your children to the path of rebellion, you can begin to bring that child home through your prayers of repentance to our heavenly Father starting immediately. Your repentance will open the doors for their repentance!

Training in Obedience

If you do not know how to confidently and lovingly lead your child through the school of obedience, this book is designed to help you get started. Yes, it will probably be difficult, but it is a lot less difficult then watching your child slip off the path of life into the devil's path of destruction.

I know in my heart that some of Kalyn's struggles in her adolescence were probably due to my rebellion to

God's ways in her early life. I regret that she didn't get from her dad or me the training in obedience she needed during her first six years. A wise teacher once taught me that the struggles with authority in our lives, not conquered in toddlerhood, become the struggles revisited in adolescence. I believe that to be true. Nevertheless, I rejoice that God's Word and His training deposited in her life during her middle childhood years did not return void as promised in Proverbs 22:6, and ultimately proved victorious in her heart and mind.

We are living in a time of great danger for our children. The path of rebellion is wide and rampant, and its destination is the pit of destruction. We parents must arise out of lethargy or anything else that's holding us back and regain charge of our own kids! No one else has that God-given authority to train them as we can train them. No one else can illustrate for them as effectively the love of the heavenly Father, which is both unconditional and just—a love that says an unqualified yes to us and an uncompromised no to sin. Our children need that security in a world gone mad. They need the assurance of our hugs and affirmations *and* the assurance of our no's and firm disciplines. They may not like it now, but later they will come back and thank us for both, as Kalyn did.

God's Word addresses this and says to us as parents:

> Sons are a heritage from the LORD, children a reward [to parents] from Him. Like arrows in the hands of a warrior are sons born in one's youth. Blessed is the man whose quiver is full of them.

They will not be put to shame when they contend with their enemies in the gates.

Psalm 127:3–5

Hear, O Israel: The LORD our God, the LORD is one. Love the LORD your God with all your heart...soul...and strength. These commandments that I give you today are to be upon your hearts. *Impress* them on your children. *Talk about them* when you sit at home and when you walk along the road, when you lie down and when you get up. Tie them as symbols on your hands and bind them on your foreheads. *Write them* on the doorframes of your houses and on your gates.

Deuteronomy 6:4–9

Discipline your son [and daughter], for in that there is hope; do not be a willing party to [their] death.

Proverbs 19:18

Train a child in the way he should go, and when he is old he will not turn from it.

Proverbs 22:6

As you can see, God's Word is clear. Our children are a sacred trust from the Lord to *us*. Since God has given them to us, He will provide us with all the wisdom necessary to disciple them if we will but ask Him and yield to His ways. If you (like Doug and me) need more resources to help you train up your children and restore order, peace, and love to your home, you are not alone! I encourage you to consult our Tools and Resources sections in the back of this book.

Stand in Your Place of Authority

Holding a proper place of leadership in the lives of our children yields the obvious benefit of an orderly, peaceful home; but it holds another benefit as well. Parents should never be tricked into laying down this benefit or giving it away to another: *You* have been given *authority* over *your* own children.

Remember that word *exousia* that we learned about in an earlier chapter? We saw that God gave Jesus authority (*exousia*) over the forces of darkness and that He has given that authority to us as His followers. We can now apply that word to the sacred charge we have as the parents of our children.

Our children were not given by God to the United States government to train. Our children were not given to the church or to the school systems to raise. While we may choose to use schools and coaches and pastors and Sunday school workers to assist us in our job, the responsibility for their lives remains with *us*. Each child was given to his or her parents and then charged with this command: "Children, obey your parents in the Lord, for this is right. 'Honor your father and mother'—which is the first commandment with a promise—that it may go well with you and that you may enjoy long life on the earth'" (Eph. 6:1–3).

This means that when our children behave with immaturity or rebellion, we have a responsibility to say no to them. When the culture, through the media, is trying to steal our children's hearts, we can say no to that influence:

"No, son, you can't go to the R-rated movie." "No, young lady, you can't have Internet access on your cell phone."

When our children try to go the devil's way instead of God's way, we have authority over them to say no: "No, son, you cannot use the car." "No, daughter, your behavior has not earned the trust of going to the mall alone."

When attacks come against your home, take a stand by faith and pray like this:

> No devil, you'll not have my children, or torment my children, or drag my children down a path of destruction. I have been given authority over them and as long as they are in my household, I have authority over your plans against their lives. For 'As for me and my household, we will serve the Lord' (Josh. 24:15).
>
> God has told me in His Word that I have been given authority to tread upon snakes and scorpions and over all the power of the enemy (Luke 10:19), and that whatever I allow on earth will be allowed in heaven and whatever I disallow on earth will be disallowed in heaven. (Matt. 18:18.) So devil, I'll let you know right now that I disallow rebellion over my household for it is as the sin of witchcraft. (1 Sam. 15:23 NKJV.) I disallow pride and bitterness. I disallow acts of sinful rebellion such as alcohol, drugs, premarital sex, and violence. I disallow tormentors such as depression, oppression, anxiety, and stress.
>
> I say no to the curse as written in Deuteronomy 28 over me and my household, but I say yes to the blessing over me and my household. I say yes to You, God, and to Your Word: I say yes to submission to authority in my life and my kids' lives. I say yes to obedience, and because of

that I say yes to all the blessings of Deuteronomy 28. I say my kids are blessed. They are protected. They are fulfilling their God-given callings and destinies. They honor their mother and father and it goes well with them all the days of their lives. (Ex. 20:12.)

As parents, we *can* say no! Our prayers and our authority have power in the spirit realm. Though we may not see our prayers answered instantly in the natural realm, they are at work in the spirit realm from the moment we make our requests and declarations. We must learn to use our position of authority now like never before!

As the battle rages over this generation, God is looking for parents who will stand in their place of authority, both in the natural and spiritual realm. Many have been tricked by secular ideas and concepts into leaving their rightful place. Then they wonder why their prayers seem ineffective. We must wake up. What *we* allow in our families God has no choice but to allow. If we allow rebellion, He will allow us to make our own choice. He is faithful to His own Word, and along with giving us a free will, He has given us authority to take our position, both as a Christian and as a parent.

I encourage you to take your God-given place of authority and stand strong in it *now*. Then as you submit yourself to God, you will have power to resist the devil—and he will flee from you! (James 4:7.)

CHAPTER 11

"An Ounce of Prevention..."

Remember how this book began with an allegory of the Journey through adolescence? The story told of a long, harrowing boat ride with a parent and his teenager, who was steering the boat, and their encounters with dangerous river islands like Drug Abuse, Alcohol, Sexual Abuse, and Rebellion. We would never think of jumping in our car to embark on a long cross-country journey without first clearing our schedule, making a plan, checking our equipment, and packing our supplies. Our Journey through adolescence with our children is an even bigger endeavor, yet many parents embark on it like it was an impromptu trip to the corner store. Consequently, the Journey takes them by surprise, and they are unprepared for what lies ahead.

With a young generation at risk, parents can't afford a "shoot from the hip" attitude to parenting. We must believe God for His grace to equip us, get prepared, and stay in a state of readiness for any twists and turns along the way. Otherwise, just like our family "boat" in the allegory (and just like the Cherry family) our boat could run aground on one of our twenty-first century "islands." Having survived both successful and disastrous "boat rides," I am more convinced than ever that along with obedience and taking our God-given place of authority as parents, we must prepare our:

- ✓ Attitude—with optimism and hope
- ✓ Spirit—with the fruits of patience, kindness, and self-control
- ✓ Mind—with accurate information on adolescent development
- ✓ Schedule—with priority and flexibility
- ✓ Marriage—with unity, love, and respect
- ✓ Environment—with teen protections and family vision
- ✓ Children—with open communication on teen struggles

Since our experience with Kalyn, Doug and I have made some changes in how we've prepared our subsequent children for their Journeys. I thought I had prepared Kalyn, but looking back I realize my preparation was inadequate and left room for someone else to gain access to her heart.

We have a new strategy—we have already determined that we want to be the "experts" that our kids seek for all their growing up questions. That goal takes more effort to achieve than I thought previously! I will need to be the one to talk with my kids about teenage developmental pressures like peer pressure, rebellion, and sexuality; and those discussions need to be *early* and *often* and *clear*. Fortunately, there are a lot of people who offer helpful resources; I've listed many of them at the end of this book, like James Dobson with his book *Preparing for Adolescence,* and Shannon Ethridge, Stephen Arterburn, and Fred Stoeker, who can help teach us how to reach our daughters and sons early through books such as *Preparing Your Daughter for Every Woman's Battle*, and *Preparing Your Son for Every Man's Battle.*

In our culture, teen pressures are coming earlier than even a generation ago, which is why we who are parents need to let our kids know that as a family we are prepared for the Journey. I consider more preparation at earlier ages necessary since kids are receiving full exposure to sexual issues almost every time they walk through the grocery check-out line or watch a TV commercial. So in this chapter I want to share some elements of the preparation process for parents that Doug and I have learned.

Join the "PIA"

A successful membership in what I call the PIA (Parent Investigating Agency) is not dependent on our ability to accomplish complicated espionage techniques, but rather it is dependent on our ability and our willingness to know our own teens and their world. To know them is to assess them as they really are—not as we wish or imagine them to be. We must know them in their strengths and weaknesses, their successes and failures. It is to know their individual personality type and how it differs from our own. Is he or she a popular sanguine (social, friendly), a powerful choleric (strong, decisive, even stubborn and arrogant), a perfect melancholy (a thinker, an evaluator), or a peaceful phlegmatic (laid back, easygoing)?[1]

Another important job we have as parents is to know the condition of our teens' spiritual state. Have they come to a point of owning their personal faith in Jesus Christ or are they mostly going through Christian motions, riding on the coattail of their parents' faith? Ideally, adolescence is the season of life designed by God to solidify personal faith and Christian worldview before teenagers step into the place of adult independence. Knowing where your child is in that process is vital. Each of our children must make their own independent, personal decision to follow Christ and believe His word. While we, as parents, can't control that which he or she must personally own and embrace, we are able to pray for God to finish His maturing work in our child's life.

To know our teens is to know their likes and dislikes, their styles and tastes. On a deeper level, to know them is to know their concerns, anxieties, wounds, and fears. To know them inside and out can seem difficult, but with God's help it is not impossible. Ask the Lord to help you open the doors of communication so you can truly hear what is in your child's heart.

When Kalyn's heart swung completely shut to us, it was horrifying. In fact, it seemed as if she was suddenly gone, yet in reality, she never went anywhere. She desperately needed parents who, under God's power, could go back after her wounded heart. Will you do what it takes to reestablish close relationship with your child? Perhaps, like us, you'll need to learn some new skills in your parenting and communicating. (See our book resource list in the Tools section.) Perhaps you'll have to believe God for a supernatural miracle. If so, you can stop right now and ask Him.

Once we know our teens, it is also our job to know our teens' world. Who are our teens' friends, their classmates, their teachers, their coaches? What are those important people saying in their lives? Where do our teens go, who are they with, and what are they doing? It's our job as parents to know!

While knowing our teens and knowing their world are both vitally important to a successful Journey, what kind of a river pilot would ever think of beginning a Journey without investigating thoroughly their river course? Wow, did Doug and I ever make some errors with this one! I thought I knew something about those dangerous river islands like Drug Abuse, Alcohol, and Rebellion, but I found out the hard way that my knowledge base was sorely lacking. As a registered nurse, I could easily spout off for you the warning signs for serious teen diseases like diabetes or bacterial meningitis. But I was totally ignorant of the warning signs of teenage Sexual Abuse or teenage Depression (other "islands" in our river Journey) until we ran ashore on those "islands" ourselves.

How many times have I wished I had known then what I know now! If you knew that your daughter had a 1-in-4 chance and your son a 1-in-6 chance of contracting a serious illness that could affect them for life, wouldn't you take the time and effort to investigate how to protect them? That's why Kalyn and I have included some educational resources at the end of this book. It's every parent's job to find out what we need to know about the current teen dangers. Still, once we know our teens and their world, there's something else we must do.

Be Alert

I'm sure most parents of teenagers have heard the common complaint, "But Mom, Dad, don't you trust me?" A wise parent can reply, "I trust you, but it's the rest of the world I don't trust." The apostle Paul must have understood about these difficult days we are living in for he wrote concerning the approaching of the return of Jesus, "Let us not be like others, who are asleep, but let us be *alert* and self-controlled" (1 Thess. 5:6). The apostle Peter wrote of the time of Jesus' return too, saying, "Prepare your minds for action; be self-controlled; set your hope fully on the grace to be given you when Jesus Christ is revealed" (1 Peter 1:13).

Alertness is a spiritual discipline that means to be fully aware and attentive, to have an attitude of vigilance, readiness, or caution, and to guard against danger. To be *alert* means to be truthful and honest in our assessments.

It means to avoid overlooking, denying, wishful thinking, or naivety; to uncover the fire when you see the smoke.

Over the years many have asked Doug and me if we saw any warning signs of the danger Kalyn was in. That's one of my most torturing questions. We know that hindsight is always 20/20 so it is still hard for me to second guess as to whether we had enough warning signs to detect the problem. But here is what I do know. We saw the smoke, but we didn't look hard enough to find the fire—and we didn't know what the fire looked like when we did see it!

I remember the day in January 2002, some eight months before our meltdown. Doug got a phone call from a co-worker of the perpetrator of the abuse who was also a mutual friend of ours from church. He had seen Kalyn chatting online with this man while the man was at work, and he was concerned about Kalyn. I remember the very strange basement meeting we had with Kalyn concerning the warning phone call. Her behavior was so odd and out of character. She was defensive of the perpetrator and strangely angry about Dad's order for her to cut off all contact with him immediately. I remember the strange darkness that fell over her face for a few seconds. I had never seen that dark look before, and wasn't to see it again until that dreadful day in October.

I remember leaving the basement and meeting with Doug in our bedroom. I was strangely shaken by our conversation so I asked him, "What was that all about?" But I don't remember us concluding that we needed further investigation, and I don't remember ever really questioning Kalyn's answers. After all, she had never lied to us before. We were confident she would obey our order to stay clear of the man whom we no longer trusted. Naivety? Denial? Maybe. Wishful Thinking? Ignorance? Absolutely.

Another incident I remember was the day in late August when I caught Kalyn coming out of the garage after doing her "quiet time" as she called it. I remember the strange rebellious-type look on her face when I questioned her about her sudden change of wardrobe. I couldn't put my finger on what was exactly different, but in recent weeks she was suddenly demonstrating a more "seductive" look. I clearly saw the smoke that day, but why, oh why, didn't I look for the fire? She had probably been on a cell phone in the garage, talking to the perpetrator just moments before. That's why the "seductive look," but I didn't see it.

Something else I remember was asking Kalyn about her obvious weight loss between July and September (another warning sign), but her answer seemed reasonable at the time. Eliminating junk food. Exercise. I even commented to Doug in September about her extra-good, extra-trying-hard, extra-special-pleasing-to-mom behavior. Did it seem like new maturity to him? Or did something about it not seem right?

One time I even was joking with Nathan about how Kalyn might not have been too interested in helping him or me or anybody else in our musical group to carry our musical equipment, but she always seemed eager to help this man and his family with all their stuff (yet another warning sign).

Then that dreadful day in October came, and it totally surprised us—that's true. But it was not without the following warning signs and symptoms, which seem to be the norm in this kind of situation:

✗ Overachievement

✗ Loss of appetite and weight loss

✗ Pseudo maturity

✗ Defensive behavior toward perpetrator

✗ Extra sleeping and daytime naps

✗ Sexual acting out seductiveness

✗ Secrecy

By God's grace never again! *God, help us to know our kids' world and constantly stay alert to hidden dangers that they cannot see.*

I didn't understand, until it happened to us, that a child or youth under the influence of a sexual predator will *almost never* tell others. I had been counting on Kalyn's willingness and ability to ask for our help if she ever needed it, but sexually abused kids rarely will. They generally have been groomed into thinking the relationship is normal. Then the abuser threatens them that if they tell, they will get in trouble. They feel helpless *in* the abuse and helpless to get *out*. So it's our job to be *alert* for them.

Teaching them to say no and resist an abuser (which we had done in Kalyn's childhood) will only work if the child recognizes the abuser as a threat instead of a trusted friend or relative. The fact is that over 95 percent of child molesters are not strangers.[2] They are trusted adults with insider status in the child's or teen's world, such as family members, family friends, teachers, or leaders. Therefore, no amount of child education can ever replace parental alertness. Remember too that what seems obviously dangerous to an adult may not seem dangerous to a teen or child.

Assured Victory

Statistics tell us that a lot of the out-of-control teens we meet every day are hiding the secret wounds of abuse. Many are hiding other secret wounds as well. All of them need parents, grandparents, youth leaders, and churches who can believe God for their healing and help them through their Journey to maturity. That's why to succeed in the Journey, we must (1) prepare ourselves and our family, (2) investigate our teen and his or her world, and (3) practice alertness (which means have a battle plan).

When a crisis hits, whether it be relatively minor or earthshakingly major, it is never a pre-planned event. The devil counts on the element of surprise to shake us off our guard. He hopes we will flounder around ineffective and without a strategy so he can gain an upper hand with his tactics. But those who are prepared with a battle plan will have what Jesus said He has given us in Luke 10:19.

I have given you authority to trample on snakes and scorpions and to overcome all the power of the enemy; nothing will harm you.

The next three chapters contain the battle plan that Doug and I learned from our parenting crisis with Kalyn. I have included it to help you prepare for whatever parenting crisis may come your way or win the victory over any that you might be in right now. These chapters embody and solidify the concepts of this message, so please don't skip them (and be sure to read the example prayer included in them) because I believe that they're the launching ground for parental preparedness in the future—and when you are prepared for the day of battle, *your victory is sure!*

CHAPTER 12

The Victory Battle Plan, Part 1

Preparing for Battle

*I*t was early spring of 2004. About a year and a half had passed since our first night of crisis. It seemed to me that so much had changed in our family. Gone were those days of subtle innocence— at least in my own mind. Yet I was smart enough to realize that most of the changes that were so obvious to me were barely noticeable to the casual observer. We were still an unusually large, well-kept family pastoring a church and driving a big white van. As I pondered how much the Lord had done to save our daughter and family from utter destruction, I was extremely grateful, but I was beginning to sense a new season was dawning. The pressure of those 18 months was producing a smoldering passion on the inside of me to share with other parents the hope that we had found in our time of crisis, and to see a generation rescued from destruction.

As I looked around I recognized that our family was not the only family embroiled in a horrible battle. Several of our precious church parishioners were struggling with various problems and issues in their families. Although my confidence level of speaking to others was still shaken, I knew it was time to reach out and help those who were in parenting struggles of their own. So one morning as I prepared to teach a Sunday school class, I grabbed a pen and paper to jot down a few notes about what I thought Doug and I had learned from our family's long ordeal. I was shocked when the Victory Battle Plan emerged on my notepad from what I'd written down within just a few short minutes.

The Lord had taught Doug and me so much about His principles of warfare—too much to think that it was only for our own help. I believe that contained within the battle plan that I began to write down that day is the hope of deliverance for every parent in need. Even now as I look at this amazing 12-step list, I am awed at how our heavenly Father, through the power of the Holy Spirit, lovingly led us through each of these critical steps—although at the time I might not have recognized them. I am amazed too at how applicable this battle strategy is for any parenting emergency, whether it be one of health, trauma, emotional turmoil, rebellion, addiction, or strife.

Some of the 12 steps have been mentioned in previous chapters; others will be new concepts. Steps 1 to 6 may be considered sequential, while 7 to 12 are not necessarily so but must be implemented only after 1 to 6 are successfully in action. When I considered how the Lord accomplished these 12 steps in our family, I discovered that some steps I revisited many times; others I lived in on a daily basis.

In the opening hours of our parenting crisis, when our emotions were undone and our thoughts were irrational, Doug and I should have intentionally applied steps 1 to 6 in order and in complete agreement with each other. It would have saved us so much time, pain, and destruction, for what you say and do in the immediate moments of initial crisis sets the stage for your family's crisis response. While God helped us eventually through all six important steps (and then the rest), our poorly chosen words of response on October 19 damaged our daughter even further. I want to show you how to avoid that kind of situation, so I'm going to take each step separately and demonstrate how to use all twelve effectively.

Step 1: Stop, Drop, and Pray

If a crisis hit your home, who or what would you look to as your first "source of salvation"—your emotions, mind, bank account, spouse, parents, pastor, sister or friend? We know, of course, that when we have time to be reasonable, each of those sources is sorely inadequate. Yet in the opening moments of a crisis, are you more self-trained to go to the phone or to the throne? The Bible tells us the best thing to do first.

In the day of my trouble I will call to you, for you will answer me.

Psalm 86:7

Times of crisis are times of intense mental, emotional, physical, and spiritual pressure. Often that pressure will try to force us into an exaggerated sense of time urgency that says, "I don't have time to pray about this. I must act *now*. I must say something *now*. I must stop this craziness *now*." In reality, however, most (but admittedly, not all) crisis scenes could be interrupted by at least a brief prayer to allow God in on the problem. Sometimes refusing to respond to a situation on the spot, in the heat of the moment, is, in fact, your best hope as a parent. Reckless words spoken can never be totally retrieved and can sometimes escalate a minor crisis into a mega crisis.

I've often wondered what the outcome would have been in our crisis if we would have paused our conversation after Kalyn came out of her lies and finally admitted to the cell phone bill. What if we had asked her to step outside our room for a few moments? We could have stopped and prayed for wisdom. We could have calmed our own emotions and received God's direction as to how to proceed with our conversation.

I know one thing for sure: God had a wise, grace-filled plan for how to respond to her humiliating disclosure. It was available from Him to us as parents, and I'm very sure that we didn't receive it. Instead, our own hasty, misinformed, reckless words pierced our daughter's heart like a sword. (Prov. 12:18.) What we needed were words seasoned with the grace of God. We needed words that would be "apples of gold in settings of silver" (Prov. 25:11), words that were totally appropriate to accomplish God's kingdom plan set in a tone and atmosphere that was bathed in love and truth. Those kinds of words will not spill out from souls that are frantic, fearful, or undone.[1]

Although we responded wrongly to Kalyn, as soon as she left our room, we fell to our knees and began crying out loud to the Lord our words of desperate need: "God, help us! Have mercy on us, Jesus! What should we do, Lord? Oh God, save our daughter!" We knew He was our only hope. We also knew He alone could deliver us from evil.

Thank God we took our pain and voiced our cry to Him. We could have turned inward and sobbed, or we could have turned on each other in anger and cried out about each other's mistakes and weaknesses—but we knew better. We knew God alone would understand and hear our hearts' cries. He alone could bear our pain.

Throughout Scripture we find many cases of people who were in trouble voicing aloud their needs to God. The children of Israel cried out during their slavery and got answered. (Ex. 2:23.) In the times of the Judges, the people would cry out to God for deliverance, and God would answer their cries. (Judg. 3:9; 4:3; 6:7.) Samuel cried out to the Lord when the Philistines were threatening to destroy Israel and God routed the enemy. (1 Sam. 7:10.) But my favorite examples are in the book of Psalms. Psalm 142, for example, was written by David when he was in a cave hiding from his enemy:

I *cry aloud* to the LORD; I lift up my voice to the LORD for mercy. I *pour out* my complaint before Him; before Him I tell my trouble. When my spirit grows faint within me, it is You who know my way. In the path where I walk, men have hidden a snare for me. Look to my right and see; no one is concerned for me. I have no refuge; no one cares for my life. I *cry to you,* O LORD; I say, "You are my refuge, my portion in the land of the living." *Listen to my cry,* for I am in desperate need; rescue me from those who pursue me, for they are too strong for me. Set me free from my prison, that I may praise Your name.

Psalm 142:1–7

Crying aloud to God did not bring instantaneous relief to our pain. We didn't just do it once on October 19 and never cry out again. But immediately at the moment of our first cries God's delivering hand was at work. He was now Lord over our situation. He was able to reach into our hearts to bring strength and hope and surround us with songs of deliverance. (Ps. 32:7.) He allowed our feet to hit the ground ready for the fight ahead.

Step 2: Calm Yourself in the Lord

Our praise and our worship of Him lift up His name above our situation and cause our soul to be quieted in His presence. When I was a child, one of my favorite hymns to sing was "My Hope Is Built,"[2] but it wasn't until recent years that I really understood the hymn writer's words: "When all around my soul gives way, He then is all my hope and stay."

A soul giving way is not a pretty sight. Emotions charge into overdrive and rational thinking goes by the wayside. King David knew how to control his own soul in times of crisis, as he said, "My soul, wait silently for God alone" (Ps. 62:5 NKJV). Learning to control our soul is a matter of spiritual discipline. We have many daily opportunities to learn to quietly (or loudly!) address our soul. In the midst of any kind of turmoil, confusion, and pressure we can say, "Soul, you wait in silence for God alone."

Our hope is based on the promises of God, and He promised in Psalm 23 to be our good shepherd and lead us "beside quiet waters" (v. 2). He promised to restore our soul, to bring it back to a place of order, rest, and peace. (v. 3.) He promised to prepare a table (a place of sustenance or feasting) before us even as our enemies are at work. (v. 5.) We can trust Him to do all of this as we claim His words of promise.

Calming yourself in the Lord is not just psychological relaxation. It is the action of receiving by faith the covenant promises of all He has purchased for us:

✓ *His peace*: "The LORD gives strength to His people; the LORD blesses His people with peace" (Ps. 29:11);

✓ *His rest*: "He who dwells in the shelter of the Most High will rest in the shadow of the Almighty" (Ps. 91:1);

✓ *His strength*: "God is our refuge and strength, an ever-present help in trouble" (Ps. 46:1);

✓ *His might*: "You are the God who performs miracles; You display Your power among the peoples. With Your mighty arm You redeemed Your people, the descendants of Jacob and Joseph" (Ps. 77:14–15).

Those promises manifest in our lives as we meditate on and speak forth His Word. (Heb. 4:12). The Word of God is our offensive weapon. When all around our soul (our mind, will, and emotions) is trying to give way, we need the Word to bring forth His promises and anchor our soul once again to the Rock.

What if during the heat of the battle, we can't even remember one Bible verse that applies to our situation? Thankfully, God has even provided for that.

> In the same way, the Spirit helps us in our weakness. We do not know what we ought to pray for, but the Spirit himself intercedes for us with groans that words cannot express. And he who searches our hearts knows the mind of the Spirit, because the Spirit intercedes for the saints in accordance with God's will.
>
> Romans 8:26,27

Praying in the Holy Spirit releases God's power into our situation. He can bring to our memory His Word (which is why scripture memory work is so valuable). Once our soul is restrained and quiet, God's mighty power working through our spirit can prepare us for the battle ahead.

Step 3: Boldly Refuse Condemnation

Remember what we've learned—that when a parenting crisis strikes, our enemy, the devil, has by some method already attacked the child; the devil is now poised to push the parents into the dark night of the soul and then pull the parents toward the pit with their child. Yet his ploys can be foiled *by resisting his actions at the onset of the battle.*

The devil's actions are revealed in verses that disclose his personal nature. In John 8:44 he is known as the *father of lies.* In 2 John 1:7 he is known as the *deceiver.* In Revelation 12:10 (NKJV) he is known as the *accuser of our brethren.* Another word for *accuse* is *condemn,* which accurately describes him because he's always trying to condemn us. Even when our own glaring parenting weaknesses and failures are screaming at us so loudly that we can hardly hear ourselves think, we must learn to boldly refuse all condemnation. It is paralyzing and does not come from God!

Condemnation is defined as "censure, blame."[3] It involves fault-finding, criticizing, and comes from the forces of darkness working on our own flesh. The condemning voice of our accuser is easy to recognize, as he speaks words like:

✗ "Your family is a failure."

✗ "You are no good."

✗ "You can't be a decent mother/father. Remember what you did?" (Or, "Remember what your mom/dad did?")

✗ "You always mess up."

✗ "God can't help people like you."

✗ "You're not going to make it through this."

✗ "This is all your fault. If you had just not done
_____, then this never would have happened."

Scriptures describe the force of condemnation as "worldly sorrow," and worldly sorrow is deadly, but "Godly sorrow brings repentance that leads to salvation and leaves no regret" (2 Cor. 7:10). Notice too the words of hope in Romans 8:1–2:

> Therefore, there is now *no condemnation* for those who are in Christ Jesus, because through Christ Jesus the law of the Spirit of life set me free from the law of sin and death.

So we can resist the force of accusation and condemnation assailing our minds by saying no to those thoughts as they first pop into our head and by *disallowing* our mind to dwell upon them.

Step 4: Welcome Godly Conviction

As we quickly raise up a *no* to condemnation, we must immediately welcome godly conviction by saying *yes* to God (conviction). In the same way that worldly sorrow and wallowing in condemnation leads to death, godly sorrow and welcoming conviction leads to life. (2 Cor. 7:10.) *Conviction* can be defined as "The act of convincing a person of error or of compelling the admission of a truth."[4] To welcome conviction we must employ the power gifts available to us that we saw earlier—brokenness, truthfulness, and forgiveness. When we do, those gifts can become our best friends.

From our posture of brokenness, we can cry out to God for His truth concerning our situation to be revealed. It is the Holy Spirit's job to convict us of our sins. (John 16:8.) So when we cry out to God, He answers by giving us His power and grace to receive the news of our sin. Then we can choose to repent of the sin that He reveals.

Many of us have never been taught how to properly repent of our sins. Perhaps we were raised in a home where the words *I'm sorry* were rarely spoken. Or maybe we learned a shallow form of repentance that says, "Hey, if I did anything wrong, forgive me." Proper repentance is so much more. True repentance of our sin involves a three-step process: 1) we agree with God that what we did was sin and was wrong, and then take responsibility for our actions; 2) we tell God we're sorry and ask Him to forgive us; 3) we turn away from our sin, forsake it, and begin to move our life in the proper direction.

As an example let's say that during this time of crying out to God, the Lord convicted you of not spending enough time with your child. Perhaps He had previously warned you about selfishly pursuing your own personal hobbies at the expense of your family. Your time of repentance might sound something like this:

Lord, I agree that I have sinned. I was selfishly pursuing my own hobbies even when You warned me of my child's needs, which was foolish and rebellious. I was wrong to disobey You and leave my child open to the devil's attack. Please forgive me. Thank You that according to 1 John 1:9 You are faithful and just to forgive me of my sins and to cleanse me of all unrighteousness. Thank You that I am free from the power of that sin. (Rom. 6:14.) I turn from the sin of selfishness and disobedience. I give all of my life totally to You and ask You to direct all my ways, including how to use my time and effort.

Lord, take back the ground that I gave up over my child's life. Thank You for the power of the blood of Jesus that is delivering us from all the evil this sin allowed. I take my place of authority in the spirit realm right now and say yes to You, God. I say no to you, devil, and I disallow your activity in my household, in Jesus' name. Thank You, Lord, for Your good plans for us. Amen.

Our proper repentance will *open* the door to God and *close* the door to the devil. Then when the devil tries to stir in your mind the remembrance of your sin, you can remind him of the remembrance of your repentance and your Father's cleansing power.

These same three proper steps of repentance are also necessary to heal relationships that have been damaged by our sin.[5] Perhaps the Lord would convict you of specific sins you committed against your child or your spouse. If so, repent first to the Lord, but then also go to that loved one and repeat those same important three steps:

<u>(Person's name)</u>, *I was wrong when I* <u>(sin you committed against them)</u>. *I am sorry. Will you please forgive me?*

Forgiveness from the Lord has already been promised us through our precious covenant promises, but forgiveness from another person can only be given us as a gift. We can't make someone else forgive us; we can't demand it. Yet when we repent, we can rest assured that the Holy Spirit will be working on the other person to convict him or her of their unforgiveness. Give the other person some time to receive God's grace and then walk in faith that your own repentance will open a door for restoration and healing.

Step 5: Declaring Your Covenant Place of Promise

This is the step where we remind *ourselves* of all the good promises that God has made to us and to our family, and we put our spiritual weapon of the sword of the spirit— the Word— into action to defeat the power of the devil's tactics. (Eph. 6:7.) God's Word is filled with wonderful promises that are made available to those who are in covenant relationship with Him (who have given their lives to Jesus and so are authorized to walk in His *exousia*). By some counts it is estimated that there are over 6,000 statements of promise contained in the Word that are available to the child of God. Those promises cover every area of our families' lives—our *health* (Isa. 53:5; Jer. 30:17), our *peace* (Isa. 26:3; 54:13), our *safety* (Ps. 4:8; Prov. 1:33), our *deliverance* (Ps. 37:24; James 4:7), our *provision* (Deut. 8:18; Phil. 4:19).

Speaking God's promises is how we declare our place of authority over our own lives. When we take and declare God's Word (His promises) out loud, it allows:

- ✓ *Our own faith in the Word to be increased.* (Rom. 10:17)
- ✓ *God's Word to divide and separate truth from lies.* (Heb. 4:12)
- ✓ *The release of the power of faith.* (Matt. 17:20)
- ✓ *God's Word to defeat the power of darkness.* (Luke 10:19)
- ✓ *The power of the Holy Spirit to perform His own Word.* (Jer. 1:12)

If you have not yet discovered the power of speaking God's Word aloud over your own life and your own situation, I want to help you to learn more about it. I have a personal scripture declaration sheet that the Lord helped me write during our family's battle. It was so helpful to us then that I wouldn't dream of laying it aside now. If I go through all of them in a morning, it takes about 15 minutes. I've included some of them in the Tools section, but you can add your own to the list. Using God's Word this way needs to be as diligent and serious as taking a doctor's prescribed medicine for an illness!

As you make declaring these scriptures an important part of each day, I believe you'll be amazed as you start seeing positive results in your life and family. Over and over again, I have experienced the power of those 15 minutes transforming the outlook on my day and opening doors for God's power to work in my life. This scriptural declaration not only transforms my mind and heals my emotions, it also transforms circumstances. I have watched God perform His own Word so many times!

～

A few weeks after God gave me this scriptural confession routine, I sensed His leading to do better at caring for my body during this season of intense stress. Months of overwhelming emotional trauma during my postpartum recovery from Lydia had left my body uncharacteristically weak. Though I've always exercised regularly, one day I decided to join a fitness center and distinctly felt the Lord's leading me to a specific one. I could get up early, leave the house and problems behind, speak God's Word during the 12-minute drive there, do my 30-minute workout, then finish speaking God's Word on the way home. The day He revealed that plan to me, I felt a new sense of hope. Getting out of the house three days a week would be worth the hour interruption of my morning routine.

My hope soon turned to anxiety, for when Kalyn heard about it, she begged to go along. Part of me was overjoyed that my depressed, lethargic, angry daughter wanted to exercise and even go with "mean old mom" to do it. But the other part of me screamed, "Oh no, it'll somehow be a mess. And I can't take any more mess!" So I told her rather emphatically, "If you go along, you'll have to drive (she had a permit), but there'll be no music or talking in the car. I'll be speaking my scriptures out loud all the way there and all the way back. So it won't be much fun for you. You'll have to sit in complete silence."

To my shock she responded, "Okay, I'll do that." I was shook! How was I going to get my rejuvenating break now? But

God had bigger plans than I did. He was busy performing His Word on our behalf, and I was so small-minded I couldn't see His plan.

After a few weeks went by, Kalyn and I were both gaining physical strength, she was amazingly quiet and respectful of my scripture prayer routine, and I was rejoicing in some surprisingly positive mother/daughter bonding time. The crowning reward of our efforts came the day I accidentally forgot my Bible and scripture sheets. I was frustrated with myself and yet determined to speak as much as I could by memory. That was the day when it dawned on me about God's bigger plan. As I stumbled to a halt with one of my scriptures, Kalyn immediately piped up and finished the verses for me. And all those weeks I thought she had been ignoring me! God got His powerful healing Word into Kalyn even when she was too weak or too defiant to do it herself. His Word would not and could not return void without accomplishing that for which it was sent. (Isa. 55:11.)

We get the power of God's Word working in our lives by asking the Lord to guide us to the scriptures specific for our situations and then personalizing them. For instance, we can pray and declare 2 Timothy 1:7 (NKJV) that says, "God has not given us a spirit of fear, but of power and of love and of a sound mind" by saying, "*I* was not given a spirit of fear, but *I* have a spirit of power and love and a sound mind."

If you are not sure you can believe the awesome good provision of God's promises (if you aren't sure you are believing what you are saying), that's all right! Just keep speaking those promises aloud until faith supernaturally begins to rise up in your spirit, and you will begin to believe the Word. Our faith comes by hearing the message, and the message is heard through the Word of Christ. (Rom. 10:17.)

I once heard someone say that it is impossible to out think the devil—but you can out talk him! Every time the devil brings an anxious, worrisome, condemning, tormenting thought to you, you can cast that thought down and replace it with the spoken Word of God. Jesus did that in His battle against Satan in the wilderness. Every time the devil brought Him a temptation, He responded aloud with, "It is written..." and then He spoke a promise from God's Word. (Luke 4.) If Jesus needed to do this during His time on earth to overcome the enemy, what makes us think we would need to do anything less?

CHAPTER 13

The Victory Battle Plan, Part 2

Building Your Strategy

The next step in the Battle Plan is powerfully illustrated in the story of Jehoshaphat, which unfolds with three enemy armies surrounding the land of Judah, ready to attack. King Jehoshaphat was very fearful and immediately sought the Lord and called for a nation-wide fast. When all of Judah's inhabitants came together, Jehoshaphat stood in their midst and cried out to God. Then the Lord sent His answer to Jehoshaphat:

> The Spirit of the LORD came upon Jahaziel...a Levite...as he stood in the assembly. He said: "...*This is what the LORD says to you*: 'Do not be afraid or discouraged because of this vast army. For the battle is not yours, but God's. Tomorrow march down against them. They will be climbing up by the Pass of Ziz, and you will find them at the

end of the gorge in the Desert of Jeruel. You will not have to fight this battle. Take up your positions; stand firm and see the deliverance the LORD will give you, O Judah and Jerusalem. Do not be afraid; do not be discouraged. Go out to face them tomorrow, and the LORD will be with you.'"

2 Chronicles 20:14–17

Notice that God spoke to His people and gave them a specific battle plan for their situation. They obeyed, sent forth praise and worship singers out ahead of the army, and the Lord intervened. The enemies ended up destroying each other, and Jehoshaphat was victorious. In that particular battle, the strategy was one of praise. In other battles, God's strategies might look a little different.

Naaman was asked to dip in a dirty river seven times, and his leprosy was cured. (2 Kings 5.) Peter was asked to cast his net on the other side of the boat and his nets were filled to overflowing with fish. (Luke 5.) Scripture is full of other instances when the Lord spoke to His people and gave them His plan—and He is still speaking to His people today. The Captain of our salvation always has a plan. (Heb. 2:10 KJV.) The real question is, will anyone seek out His plan, listen to His instructions, and dare to obey them?

"He, who loved you unto death, is speaking to you" wrote Amy Carmichael, a well-known missionary to India for 55 years. "Listen, do not be deaf and blind to Him. And *as you keep quiet and listen*, you will know, deep down in your heart...." She revealed an important clue on hearing from God—*keep quiet and listen*.[1] That's a major part of Step 6. I know it's true from our crisis with Kalyn—once I was able to get to a quiet place where I could hear God speak to my heart, it made all the difference between victory and defeat.

Step 6: Receiving Your Battle Strategy from the Lord

It was December 2002, two months into our crisis. When I look back, I see us all living in a strange thick fog. Kalyn was angry, mean, defiant, and hostile one minute and then weepy, sullen, and withdrawn the next. It was, to put it mildly, a mess.

After our first phone consultation with Focus on the Family's counselors, we had followed their advice and consulted a local Christian counselor. He was a wonderfully kind man who listened to our story and then worked with both Doug and me and then Kalyn. Yet somehow through that process we made no progress, and he suggested we seek another solution. Kalyn refused to talk with him about anything deeper than the weather. She denied that anything at all had happened with this man, and she presented herself as a defiant teen in a stubborn state of rebellion. So for a very strange season of time we were thrown off track and focused ourselves on getting help for a rebellious teen.

Looking back I can't understand why we didn't get some crisis help for the sexual abuse, but I have to remember how confusing our presentation appeared: Kalyn thought her problem was us, and not the man; both she and the man denied anything sexual had happened in their conversations; no one besides Doug and I had witnessed all the ranges of her crazy behavior swings; and not many people are skilled at decoding the confusing aftermath of sexual abuse trauma in a teen, including its usual shroud of denial.

Some days I wondered if I could hold the house together at all. Each day I grasped for a new plan. How was I to care for a newborn, a toddler, two preschoolers, and five school-age kids—one of which didn't have the will to live? Kalyn was losing weight at an alarming rate and looked horrible so I'd let her eat anything she chose. She didn't come to family meals and lived in her room secluded, but at least once a day she would stomp down the hall to the kitchen, angrily grab a pan, shove it into the sink to fill it with water, and slam it on the stovetop. If one of the kids stared at her theatrical macaroni-cooking sprees, she'd shout back angrily, "What are you staring at!"

After a few weeks of this strange madness, we reduced our potential areas of conflict to a bare minimum (for Kalyn's sake as well as the rest of us) by rearranging bedrooms to give Kalyn her own room, moving her daily schoolwork location to Doug's office, removing all family chores and babysitting responsibilities from her, and pulling her back from any outside-the-house job commitments like at church—and still our lives were a nightmare. I was in the full swing of the dark night of a mother's soul, Kalyn was in the pit, and unless we got a new strategy soon, Doug could see I was headed to the pit with her with a house full of kids in tow. So we made call after call looking for help.

It was Christmas school break and we had to have a new school plan for January. We considered every available option—enroll her in a local private Christian school, a public school, or send her to a boarding school for behavior problem girls. It is still shocking to me that we seriously considered that last option, but this way out seemed reasonable to me! We still didn't really understand what our problem was, so our solutions seemed rather ridiculous in hindsight. Me, send my child to boarding school? I hadn't even sent her across town to kindergarten! But desperate times can sometimes cause us to reach for desperate solutions. So Doug kept looking for an "out" for us.

The Power of Seeking the Lord

We knew we only had a few days left to make our New Year school plan, but Doug wisely decided to send me on a little "relaxation" trip before we pressed through to make our decisions. I left the kids and Doug behind, packed my bags and the baby's bags and headed up to the St. Louis area to check into the Drury Inn. I knew this was supposed to be a "vacation," but I had my own kind of "work" to do. I desperately needed to spend some time with my heavenly Father. On my way to the car, I grabbed my Bible and filled my bag with worship CDs and piles of Christian books from my shelves that I thought might contain some wisdom for the hour. I must have been quite a sight hauling all that stuff plus all my baby equipment through the hotel lobby!

I sensed the Lord's presence with me from the time I stepped into my car. In the privacy of my own car and my own hotel room, my tears of pain flowed freely. But something was distinctly different about those tears. As they flowed out, rivers of God's healing love flowed in. For the first time in weeks, my soul was quieted enough to distinctively hear His still, small voice inside my heart. He strengthened me with His power and encouraged me with His hope. I heard His voice of instruction to abide in Him and rest as I read Secrets of the Vine by Bruce Wilkerson.[2] I felt my heart filled with a new load of compassion for Kalyn and a new commitment to pray for her as I read Rees Howells: Intercessor by Norman Grubb.[3]

One night I stopped at a bookstore to do some research on teenage sexual abuse and was shocked by what I found. Although Kalyn at that time still adamantly denied that anything sexual in tone had happened in those middle of the night phone calls, I had never really believed her denials. Now I had the circumstantial evidence to suggest she might be lying. As I studied the literature, I was shocked to realize that Kalyn was indeed displaying classic post-abuse trauma symptoms. I knew that we had became so distracted and consumed by the tyranny of her urgent problems of rebellion and depression that we were being distracted from understanding her true root causes—the abuse.

I studied long enough to discover the magnitude of our problem. Literature on teen sexual abuse was much more difficult to find than literature on child sexual abuse. This, after all, is an age when sexual scenes in the media and sexual experimentations among teens are considered common, if not normal. So how could a mostly phone and Internet relationship produce such damage? Wouldn't he have to have physically touched her for it to be truly called sexually abusive?

When I read sections of Dr. Dan B. Allender's classic book on sexual abuse, The Wounded Heart, *I suddenly began to understand the nature of our battle.*

> "There is a deep reluctance to begin the process of change by admitting that damage has occurred...Sexual abuse is any contact or interaction (visual, verbal, or psychological) between a child/adolescent and an adult when the child/adolescent is being used for the sexual stimulation of the perpetrator or any other person...There are two broad categories of abuse: sexual contact and sexual interactions...The categories imply a continuum of severity, but all inappropriate sexual contact is damaging and soul-distorting. Seventy-three percent of the least-severely abused victims report some damage, and 39 percent report considerable to extreme trauma as a result of past abuse...Verbal abuse is a powerful and deep wound. Sexually abusive words produce the same damage as sexually abusive contact. Yet the potential for minimization or feeling weird for being damaged makes the potential for change even more difficult for those more subtly abused than for those more severely abused."[4]

The words finally sank deep into my heart: our daughter had been sexually abused. Clearly, fourteen- and fifteen-year-old girls are not equipped to recognize and handle the psychological pressures of sexual predator behavior, hence, the breakdown in her behavior that we experienced. I was jolted to realize I had begun to view my precious, bleeding daughter like

I might a common juvenile delinquent as I had been filled with disgust, scorn, disapproval, and anger towards her.

God was giving me a glimpse into a world I had never really understood before. I suddenly realized that many of those repulsive juvenile delinquents I had encountered were really like my own daughter—hard, rebellious, and difficult because they are covering up wounded, bleeding hearts. That day I knew that it was time to shake off the dark night of my soul, roll up my sleeves, and get to work on the right frontline of this battle. Enough self-searching and analysis paralysis.

My journal writings of December 29 and 30 reflected my new understandings that "the devil is the enemy—not Kalyn, not me, not Doug. The devil's trying to destroy us all in each of our areas of weakness—it's time to turn on him, not each other."

Then God did an amazing thing for me. He began to lay out a battle plan for the next season of our family's Journey. His diagnosis and plan proved to be incredibly accurate.

As I share my journal writings, please note that the "conversation" below is my perception of what the Lord spoke to me that day. It is with great humility that I would attempt to "quote" God. However, I am including my interpretation of His instructions in this manner to help you as the reader understand that God can give us specific help when we ask.

Lisa's Journal—December, 2002

(This is the actual entry from my journal that day.)

"Lord, what are we to do?" I asked.

"Cut it off! Let Me pursue," He said.

My response to Him: *"I can see it, Lord. You did not cause this. It's an attack from the enemy, but You will use this for good in our lives. I must give her over to this season of her life to kill off the root of rebellion—to God, His Word, and earthly authorities."*

This trial is also a season of pruning for Doug and for me. I've tried complaining, rebelling, compromising, and running away. This pruning is about me placing upon the altar (or allowing to be killed off in me):

- *A "perfect family image"*
- *My kids being perfect, mature, high achievers for my glory*
- *My self-sufficiency*
- *My motherhood ambitions as a source of significance*
- *My ministry as a source of my significance*
- *My right to know, reason, and control timing and seasons of life*
- *My family's and friends' approval, understanding, or help*
- *My allowing "individuating" without fear of change (i.e. development of each child's individual identity)*
- *My trusting in God to send His Fire to my children*
- *My personal needs for love, acceptance, or approval from Kalyn— or my other children.*

Instruction from the Lord: *"We must have No Compromise—No Fear—No Condemnation."*

What we could not accomplish in her—God will accomplish. We must not "go down to Egypt" for help. We must lay it out for her (renounce worldly counsel) and help her to understand the teen year challenges she is in and that we understand and recognize her pain but hold fast to only one relief valve—God's Word and His ways. Just as what Kalyn was looking for in that man could only be found in Jesus, what I'm looking for in "calling Doug" can only be found in Jesus!

Growing edge to learn from the Lord:

- In issues of style, preference, give her room

    vs.

- In issues of modesty and vision and godly direction, give her no room

She is in an identity crisis. An identity crisis is always a spiritual crisis.

Then I sensed God speaking these words to me: "See her as delivered. See her as set free. Treat her as such. Pray the prayer of faith. Ignore symptoms. Walk in wisdom concerning the day to day. Watch My Word performed in your midst. The victory is yours, the battle is Mine. Quit battling and walk it out. Go to Higher places.

"Declare and decree My Word. It is your intercession. Receive the flow of love. Fight the battle, as you have already been prepared. Cancel the negative words over Kalyn. She is an obedient child. Celebrate each moment of victory. Encourage her whole heart. This is a cancer in her soul.

This is the picture I saw:

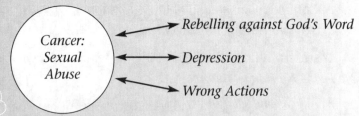

Cut off the metastasis of the cancer—false counsels, false relationships, false teachings."

I asked the Lord: *"Why did she develop the cancer?"* He answered me: *"She had a weak immune system: Her love tank is low from Mom and Dad. She feels a root of rejection from Mom. She feels low self-esteem. This is a spiritual crisis with identity confusion and rebellion not dealt with— also envy and jealousy.*

"Many of these weaknesses are developmental: i.e. adolescent brain immaturities, growing up issues, faith development issues, and individuation. But some are wounds like rejection from the abuse. Pray for healing over these wounds. Some are sin such as rebellion and envy. Strengthen her immune system now: her spirit identity, her love from God and parents. Take control over a child. Be her outer control until her inner controls have healed. Protect her from herself, from attracting others who are dangerous. Protect her emotionally.

"Prepare for Me to do a surgical removal of the cancer [the abuse wound]*—it needs precision accuracy. It needs skill. Learn so you can intercede with her in her present sense of reality. This was abuse of a child so it is very complicating to her current and future development. Let her build a new life."*

A new hope dawned in my soul. God truly did have our plan of escape marked out for us. He did know what we should do, and He did have the ability to break through my hysteria with His plan. How could I have ever doubted? The sexual abuse was at the foundation of our problem, but it was facilitated by an unchecked root of rebellion. I could see it and could now truly understand about seeking the Lord for our battle plan. We had become like Jehoshaphat when he was surrounded by enemy armies and learned the power of seeking the Lord for His battle plan.

Building a New Life

I knew that day when I drove home from my personal retreat that the next step in implementing our plan would not be easy. Keeping Kalyn at home and protecting her (cutting off the metastasis of the cancer as God said) seemed almost as impossible to me as marching around a tightly shut up city! But I knew that I must obey God's plan. So when I got home, I reported my revelations to Doug. He agreed that we should continue to home school her, but then he asked me a protecting question, "Are you sure you can do this?" I knew God deposited His grace in my heart as I heard myself answer, "Yes, with God's power."

So it went with every step of our battle plan. We asked God, we waited, we received, and then we obeyed Him. At times the plan looked logical, other times it didn't. Sometimes my own anxiety would overtake me, and I would frantically cry out to Doug, "What are we going to do now?" He would repeat his well-rehearsed speech. "We are going to ask the Lord for wisdom and do the very next thing He tells us to do."

Sometimes we followed our best "heart felt" leading by faith and sometimes God would supernaturally give us a word of wisdom. Like the day when I was seeking the Lord once again for a personal counselor for Kalyn and I heard the words in my heart, "Joyce Meyer's Emotional Healing Kit."[5] I suddenly remembered I had heard years prior of such a resource from Joyce Meyer's ministry. I was so excited to discover the kit still existed and contained 23 hours of Joyce's best teachings on emotional healing, including Beauty for Ashes. *But how would I ever get Kalyn to listen? Immediately God answered me. I was still her teacher! This would be her required curriculum for her high school Bible course. Miraculously, what started as a reluctant assignment to her became her lifeblood, as she would pour over those tapes by the hour until she began preaching their messages back to me!*

God would graciously work to comfort us and confirm His voice of instruction so it would be easier to obey. Sometimes the instruction we thought we were hearing did not line up with the popular advice we were receiving from friends, family, and even some professionals. In fact, I had to constantly remind myself that while all those people truly meant well and wanted to help and while all their solutions could have some credence as being a possible solution, only Doug and I were anointed by God as Kalyn's parents to sort through the available options for the God-ordained kingdom plan.

I can remember the horrible process we went through even after I went off on my retreat and did my best to hear the voice of the Lord. When I got home, we faced even more pressure to give in to Kalyn's demands to go to school. Part of me still wanted to agree, but deep down, I had no peace about her going. Her ability to stay out of trouble and away from the wrong crowd was nonexistent. She was normally an A student, but her ability to concentrate and learn course content was now severely limited. I felt in my heart that if we let her go right then, she could be gone for life. But what if I was hearing God wrong? *my mind would scream. You talk about a faith test!*

So God in His mercy gave us another word of confirmation. Since we had been greatly helped in the first week of our crisis by calling Focus on the Family counseling service, I, in desperation, decided to call them back. This time I briefly relayed our situation, our long-term need for a female professional counselor for Kalyn, and our current need for a schooling solution for her. The counselor's response shocked me.

That very kind man responded with an amazingly succinct, clear plan. He explained that he was very familiar with the dynamics of a home-schooling family. Since Kalyn's heart had been stolen away from her primary life support system (her parents) and her school peers (her brothers and sisters), sending her out now to another school system could be a big mistake. He ended his conversation with a very impassioned plea. He said, "Ma'am, it sounds like your daughter

desperately needs to get her heart back home before she can success-
fully launch out to a new group of peers. She needs her family's love,
and it won't be easy. Have you considered that perhaps, for right now,
you and your husband could be her best counselors?"

When I hung up the phone, I stood in holy awe. The counselor
had just confirmed everything I felt the Lord had spoken for us to do.
A deep peace hit my heart as tears flooded my eyes. "Yes, Lord, as
hard as this seems to be, I will obey," I prayed.

When we told Kalyn about our decision, she responded by getting
angry and running away. Well, God warned me it wouldn't be easy!
Minutes stretched into hours, and we didn't know where she had
gone. I willed myself to stand strong in faith and not give way to
panic. I knew my faith in God's direction was being tested. So I
continued teaching the other children and waiting for her return. Just
minutes before we were going to call the police she turned up in the
basement, cold and weepy from her day in the chilly January woods.

Looking back on that miserable day, I am in awe of God's
amazing grace—His grace to give us an answer to a very difficult
question; His grace to hold firm to our decision when that decision
was tested; His grace to enact a school plan with a miserably reluc-
tant student. Yet, I am totally convinced that our act of obedience in
keeping her home was a critical turning point in our battle. Her
heart would return home. Miraculously. And in God's perfect timing.
We needed God's specific plan for our specific needs.

You can be encouraged in the Lord that no matter
what kind of battle you could ever face in your home, God
has a plan for your victory. It will be unique and individual to your particular situation. It will be filled with
wisdom and seasoned with His grace. And it will work!

CHAPTER 14

The Victory Battle Plan, Part 3

Fighting to Win

The unfolding of our parenting crisis exactly coincided with the same month when a door miraculously opened to purchase a building that would become our church's first permanent home after four years of rented meeting rooms. It could have been a coincidence, but I don't believe it was. We were faced with a decision to bid on a building while I was deeply tempted to shut down the whole ministry.

Our earthly life battles are actually a picture of a greater battle being waged in the heavenlies: "Our struggle is not against flesh and blood, but against the rulers, against the authorities, against the powers of this dark world and against the spiritual forces of evil in the heavenly realms" (Eph. 6:12). Clearly, to win these battles we must incorporate into our lives the 12 steps I discovered during our crisis with Kalyn. So let's continue with the second half of this battle plan, starting with praying our way to victory.

Step 7: Fight on Your Knees and Act in Love

I have never considered myself to be a "prayer expert." Sometimes during the intensity of our struggles my own mind would scream, *You don't know how to pray right anyway!* But I knew that was a lie. Jesus left us a model for prayer in Matthew 6 in what is known as the Lord's Prayer, and the Holy Spirit has promised to lead us into effective prayer (Rom. 8:26), so I know I am well equipped. Everyone else is too who's hooked up to their power supplies—*exousia*, *dunamis*, and *agape* love (from chapter 7).

I can go into my room, close the door, cry out, weep, and ask, and God will always respond. I can boldly pray with my scripture promises and receive God's wisdom and power and know my covenant with Him will hold. That's what I call fighting on our knees, but each day we must decide to do it. Will I take the time and energy to seek God and pray or will I try to run on yesterday's strength? Will I turn a deaf ear to my accuser (the devil) and trust my Father's leading, or will I give up and seek the comfort of people first? Will I let the Lord develop my prayer skills and my own unique prayer style, or will I compare myself to others around me, be intimidated, and quit?

We must learn to fight on our knees—walk humbly, walk boldly, pray quietly, pray loudly, just pray—and God will respond!

There were days I spent some forceful times in prayer in my bedroom. Yet as I turned the doorknob to exit my room and reenter my family room, God would remind me (in my heart), *You've fought in prayer, now go act in love. For My love never fails.*

My children desperately needed my reassuring hugs and kind words. My daughter Kalyn especially needed my smiles and my warm motherly words of encouragement. Doug was amazing at this strategy. I would watch him tell Kalyn a tough, loving no and go right on and say, "Honey, let's go get some ice cream. It'll be fun." Then he would reach out and hug her defiantly stiff body. He wouldn't let her go. He was going to fight on his knees and then act in love—and I chose to follow his lead.

Step 8: Recapture/Hold Your Child's Heart

I am so grateful that years ago Doug and I had heard a powerful message from a man named Dr. S. M. Davis, who had nearly lost his own son to rebellion. His message was titled, *How to Win the Heart of a Rebel*. He talked about the radical measures he used to win back his child's heart after losing that heart to teen influences. He took a leave of absence from his job, put his son in the car with him, and headed on a cross-country trip. After weeks of constant togetherness with no other influential voices available, God mended their broken relationship and turned the heart of that father back to his son and the heart of the son back to the father. (See Mal. 4:6.)

Doug's immediate response to Kalyn's meltdown was so painful for me to hear. "I've lost her heart," he cried amidst sobs of pain. Having worked so hard to capture and hold Kalyn's heart throughout her childhood, I knew how deeply he felt the sting of those words. Doug had taught others so frequently on the vital importance of a father—and a mother—holding onto a child's heart until that heart was able to be transferred to their heavenly Father and to their life partner at marriage. And now Kalyn's heart was stolen.

I felt the pain with him. But at the same time deep inside me I felt hope, for my husband had already decided before October 19, 2002 that he would *never* permanently lose one of his kids' hearts. So I knew the final chapter of our life story had not yet been written. Doug would do whatever it took to recapture her heart—extra phone calls, trips to the mall, little notes of encouragement, lunch dates, hugs and pats on the back, little "I'm thinking of you" prizes, hours of time together, and even a trip to Florida.

Doug had always been so close to his daughter that her rejecting looks, abrasive comments, and sullen silences were piercing to his heart. Still, he persevered day after day, week after week. She was worth the priority. Even if it cost him in his career and finances, she was worth it. He would win her over to life by his persistent display of steadfastness and love, and at the same time he would tell her no when necessary. His love had to mirror the Father's perfectly balanced love: completely unconditional and completely just. Doug didn't always achieve his goals perfectly. Yet he continued day in and day out until God's principle of fighting on your knees and acting in love worked in our home, and he was able to eventually recapture her heart. (The book *Recreate* by Ron Luce is an excellent resource to help us learn how to woo our kids' hearts back to us.)

If we don't make the time, sacrifice the energy, and develop the priority to recapture our child's heart, who or what will hold their heart? The media? The boyfriend? The mall? Where will their heart allegiances lead them? We must go after their hearts *now*.

Step 9: Recognize and Celebrate All Victories

My fantasy continued for weeks and months. I imagined it much like the amnesia victims in the movies. One day Kalyn would somehow snap to her senses, rush to my bedroom and shout, "Mom, I can see it now! I can't believe I was so blinded. Will you help me get out of this mess?" Then our family would sit down together and joyfully celebrate the end of the battle.

My fantasy sometimes brought me comfort, but more frequently it only brought me more frustration. Instead of an instantaneous, miraculous breakthrough like I wanted, we had to learn to recognize and celebrate each piece of victory when it came. Somehow we had to be content with our day-to-day progress without selling out short on our ultimate goal: complete restoration and complete deliverance. Then we had to hold on to our faith when we didn't even experience progress.

Sometimes we experienced setbacks, like the day in August 2003 when we felt Kalyn had progressed to a point where we could release her to take an extra computer class at our local junior college. We stumbled through our day of school registration only to have Kalyn blow up at me when we got home, get on her bike, and run away. We hadn't seen that erratic behavior for months. I was tempted to cancel all plans of promotion for her indefinitely until I discovered that she had just that week noticed her own progress and decided, without consulting us, to try to come off of her antidepressant medication cold turkey. You can't do that with the kind she was taking without risking serious erratic behavioral side effects. So, we had to face the setback, draw courage from the Lord, and get back on our course to victory.

Step 10: Get Proper Support

God does not expect us as believers to live isolated lives, meeting life challenges and flying our missions solo. Although He expects us to be equipped (with the armor He's provided for us) to stand alone against all anti-Christ forces (Eph. 6:11–19), He calls us His body (the body of Christ, the church) and expects us to work together in unity. Paul makes this truth clear for us in his letter to the Corinthians.

Now the body is not made up of one part but of many. ...If one part suffers, every part suffers with it; if one part is honored, every part rejoices with it. Now you are the body of Christ and each one of you is a part of it.

1 Corinthians 12:14,26,27

In the body of Christ, we are to bear one another's burdens as an expression of our love for the head of our body, our Lord Jesus Christ. (Gal. 6:2.) When the Cherry family fell into crisis, many within the body of believers expressed a desire to bear our burden. For those expressions of love, we are eternally grateful. Some of our closest family and friends offered practical help—casseroles, babysitting, notes of encouragement. Others offered spiritual help by praying for us and offering us words of insight and counsel. We were deeply touched by their sincerity and steadfastness.

During that season I learned a lot about receiving and giving help in times of crisis. I learned that while crisis increases our need for others, it can also decrease our willingness or ability to receive their help. I know my own emotional turmoil caused me to want to run away from people and hide. I was confused, embarrassed, tormented with self-doubt, and over-emotional. I was well aware that my perceptions were faulty, and I desperately didn't want to hurt anyone else.

To make matters worse, I couldn't tell others what was really happening because Kalyn was incredibly embarrassed and volatile about her situation. So sometimes the help or advice offered was sincerely meant to help, but it was, in reality, way off base. At times the words, unbeknown to the speaker, were actually used by the devil to bring further pain and condemnation to me because my inner state, back then, was one of continual condemnation. Consequently, I found myself "over-armored" to deflect what felt like hurtful words—and that can be a dangerous state for relationships.

Something else I quickly learned was the importance of evaluating all practical and spiritual help before I accepted it in my heart. Not everyone who offered to counsel or pray with Kalyn or us was a God-appointment. We had to learn to give those situations to the Lord and quickly receive His best wisdom for how to handle each one. I had to realize that while I desperately needed to let others pray for me, I was not obligated to receive all that they said as truth. God was very gracious to give me an inner witness to those ideas that did come from Him. (See Dan. 2:20–21.)

During our quest for help we also had to learn the vital skill of evaluating the professional help we received. We consulted with many types of services by phone, but we actually made visits to three different professional counselors (before the Lord led *us* to be Kalyn's counselors). I have no doubt that all three of those counselors meant well in their desire to help others. Yet none of them proved to be *the* answer we were desperately searching for. Nevertheless, we had to be willing, in each case, to sort through their words to receive pieces of the answers that we needed.

It seemed as though we were trying to reconstruct a giant jigsaw puzzle that had blown apart. We couldn't get the whole thing back together without being willing to receive the pieces back one at a time as the Lord made them available. We also had to reject the pieces offered that were not a part of our solution.

The first Christian counselor we visited (I talked about him previously) very kindly listened to our story and brought reassurance to us that we had not totally blown it as parents. He had seen many kids go through serious adolescent crisis and still come through to maturity. We needed his perspective to give us hope! Yet he wasn't able to help us diagnosis the sexual abuse trauma response or to unlock Kalyn's denial state. So his ability to help over the long haul was severely limited.

The second counselor we visited was a nightmare experience.

A Horrifying Evaluation

One day a few months into Kalyn's crisis I entered her room to check on her and found her in bed, depressed, with all the covers over her head. Lying on the floor beside her was a notebook titled, "When Kalyn Dies." All that week, she constantly left that notebook out for us to see. Daily she made horrible, dark, frightening entries in her journal about her wish to die, and other warped emotions she had about us and this man.

Doug and I wrestled as to what to do. We began following up counseling leads to no avail and strongly considered taking her to the emergency room and doing a psychiatric screening. But we knew where that could end— the local psychiatric hospital for adolescents. We didn't want that, so we continued to make calls until a secular psychologist agreed to see us. We were grateful to get an emergency suicide evaluation before we had to suffer through the weekend—but this turned out to be a horrible visit.

After chatting with us briefly and taking the forms he had us fill out when we arrived, he sent us out to the waiting room while he talked alone with Kalyn. When he called us back in, he gave us his diagnosis: moderately severe clinical depression, but no immediate suicide threat. That was good news! The rest of his evaluation was horrifying—he believed that Kalyn would likely be in this depressed state until she was old enough to leave our house, unless we made some serious changes in our beliefs. We had cut her off from her favorite friendship and the loss of that relationship plus our "oppressive home environment" was the source of her depression. This man in a crazy way seemed to agree with Kalyn's deception! No wonder she was smiling as we came in!

In shock, I questioned his response to this sordid relationship and his answer chilled me to the bone: He would need more information before deciding if continuing that relationship was a problem; but he was confident that if we'd start to bring Kalyn to see him, he could be of some help to her. I immediately wondered what kind of help this 40-something man had to offer! I had never faced such an urge to hurt someone. Doug sensed my emotions and immediately stepped in. He politely told the counselor that we wouldn't be bringing Kalyn back. Then we calmly wrote our check and got out of there.

Kalyn was mad at us for a new reason. She liked the counselor and his ideas and wanted to continue seeing him. To her we were bad parents because we wouldn't let her!

While that counselor got inside Kalyn's head far enough to help us know that she really didn't have an active suicide plan, the visit cost us dearly in our credibility in Kalyn's eyes. Clearly, he was not God's ordained plan for help!

Line Up with God's Strategy

Counselor #3 was a skilled Christian counselor, who specialized in adolescent issues and came on high referral. He was horrified at counselor #2's conclusions and was eager to help us. He suggested we get a copy of *Yes, Your Teen Is Crazy* by Dr. Michael Bradley[1] right away. The book did not espouse Christian ideas, but it explained teen crisis reasoning and behaviors and really helped us to understand some of Kalyn's struggle.

This counselor did a good job of evaluating our situation but once again some of his conclusions fell off base. He counseled us to immediately get her on antidepression medication, which we did. He also counseled us to enroll her in school and allow her to do more "new things" that she was expressing a desire to do. His conclusion was that her root issue was a case of teenage rebellion so we should treat that first and then eventually work her out of a desire for the 46-year-old man. Some of what he said I could see was true. But he still didn't seem to understand anything about a sexual abuse trauma diagnosis and how those symptoms would interact with her rebellion and depression issues. So we took what help we could gain from our visits and left the rest behind.

I'm not saying that I wouldn't recommend counseling when faced with a crisis. I've watched many people receive great help from counseling, and I have recommended it to others in need. Yet I believe that counseling has to be from a Christian perspective and should only be used as it lines up with God's specific battle strategy for your particular battle. God just had another way for Kalyn to receive her counsel.

I encourage anyone in a crisis to receive all the help that God has to offer. Let Him use His body of believers to bring you healing and hope, but have the courage to politely refuse the "help" that is not from Him and still bless those who offer it. When you are not sure which is which, trust Jesus to sort it out and show you.

Step 11: Stay in Your Place of Authority

We've already covered this in depth, but I want to emphasize again to stay in your place of authority as a parent. The reason is that in a parental crisis parents will be tempted so often to step out and let someone else take their place: the counselor, doctor, teacher, friend, "experts," pastor, relative, child.

Remember, no one can effectively take a parent's place. Only you are anointed by God to be Dad or Mom to your child. God will give you His *exousia* (His authority), and His *dunamis* (His power), and His Agape (His love) when you will but stay in your place and ask.

Step 12: Walk in Faith and Patience

It is absolutely critical to walk by faith if we are to receive the promises of God. Receiving from God by faith is not the same as just positive thinking or hopeful wishing. *Faith* is the spiritual force of believing and trusting in God; when properly exercised according to Mark 11:22–24, faith can move mountains.

I like Joyce Meyer's commentary on these verses in her *Everyday Life Bible*:

> "Usually when we have mountains in our lives we talk *about* them, but God's Word instructs us to talk *to* them, as we see in Mark 11:22–23.
>
> "First of all, what do we say to the mountains in our lives? It is obvious that we should not hurl our will at them; we are to hurl *God's will* at them— and His will is His *word*.
>
> "Speaking the Word of God is powerful and absolutely necessary in conquering our mountains. However, it is only the beginning. Obedience is equally important. If a person thinks he can live in

disobedience, but speak God's Word to his mountains and get results, he will be sadly disappointed, as Jesus clearly stated in this passage."[2]

So what exactly is Bible-believing faith? I think the *Amplified Bible* version of Hebrews 4:3 helps us to understand: "We who have believed (*adhered to and trusted in and relied on God*) do enter that rest." True faith, then, is an adhering to, trusting in, and leaning upon God.

Notice the object of our faith is to be God—not our own faith. I'm reminded of this daily when I meditate on Psalm 91, which says in verse 4: "He will cover you with his feathers, and under his wings you will find refuge; *his faithfulness* will be your shield and rampart [or 'protective barrier']." God does the work, I do the trusting, the leaning, and the obeying; and "by faith" the promises of God are realized.

There are enemies of our faith, but we can recognize them. It's not that hard to recognize faith robbers when we understand the opposite forces of faith are *fear*, *doubt*, and *unbelief*. When these three are annihilated from the believer's life, faith will flourish.

We can't afford one day of fear. Billy Joe Daugherty, former pastor of Victory Christian Center in Tulsa, summed it up when he wrote, "*Fear* attracts the works of the *enemy*, but *faith* draws the *power of God*. Faith is a trust, an assurance in God's ability to take you through whatever He sends your way. Faith works exactly opposite of fear. Whereas fear is negative, faith is positive."[3]

To be ready for any kind of challenge, *intentionally* grow your faith much like bodybuilders grow their own muscles—by repetitive use against increasing resistance. Bodybuilders don't get strong by thinking about lifting weights; they get strong by lifting those weights! In the same way, Christians grow strong in faith by taking God's promises and applying their faith until those promises are made manifest in their lives.

Faith is a key ingredient to receiving God's promises, but faith alone will not be enough. Hebrews 6:11–12 warns us: "We want each of you to show this same diligence to the very end, in order to make your hope sure. We do not want you to become lazy, but to imitate those who through *faith* and *patience* inherit what has been promised."

Patience must have its perfect work just as faith must have its perfect work. (See James 1:4 KJV.) So we may have to wait for God's appointed timing. Not many of us enjoy waiting, but waiting patiently is exactly what God expects. That's why in Galatians 5:22 He included *patience* (or as the *King James Bible* renders the word, "long-suffering") in the fruits of the Spirit. By His Spirit in us we can wait for God's perfect will to manifest.

I believe that *patience* is the most often overlooked part of the Christian's armor. After we're instructed in the Word to put on the full armor of God (the belt of truth, the helmet of salvation, the breastplate of righteousness, the shoes of the preparation of the gospel of peace, the shield of faith, the sword of the spirit, and prayer), then we are instructed to *stand* our ground and to *stand* firm.

(Eph. 6:13–14.) In other words, we're to wait patiently while God is at work and to never give up. In our battle during the crisis with Kalyn, we needed great faith and patience for our miracle to come!

I believe that the kinds of situations requiring the most dedicated application of faith and patience involve three of the biggest challenges: 1) outbursts of erratic human behavior; 2) long, complicated processes; and 3) incomplete results. Doug and I found during our parenting crisis that all three have the capability of shipwrecking our faith and patience.

The continual pressures we faced to hold on in faith while experiencing those three biggest challenges can be seen in the next chapter, which contains Kalyn's account of her remarkable journey home. As you read this miracle testimony watch for the evidences of our 12-Step Victory Battle Plan in action. Enjoy reliving God's three-in-one power and be encouraged—He is still in the miracle-working business!

12-Step Victory Battle Plan

(clip and save for review)

1. Stop, Drop, and Pray
2. Calm Yourself in the Lord
3. Boldly Refuse Condemnation
4. Welcome Godly Conviction
5. Declare Your Covenant Place of Promise
6. Receive Your Battle Strategy from the Lord
7. Fight on Your Knees and Act in Love
8. Recapture/Hold Your Child's Heart
9. Recognize and Celebrate All Victories
10. Get Proper Support
11. Stay in Your Place of Authority
12. Walk in Faith and Patience.

CHAPTER 15

The Road Home

Even in my (Kalyn) darkest hour the light was always present; in my loneliest moment, I was never truly alone. The Lord had never left me, but had been there all along. I had given up on Him, but He never gave up on me. Could there be hope after all? Could God take this broken vessel and use it once again? Three events along my road to recovery were key; I'll never forget the first of these.

It was a sunny day in July 2003, and I had agreed to go to lunch with my dad. We had just ordered ice cream and were now sitting in the Dairy Queen parking lot. These lunch outings with Dad occurred periodically and usually ended in an explosive battle of wills and emotions. This day, however, something was different. Though I would never have admitted it, something inside of me had changed—and my dad stumbled upon it.

As we sat eating Blizzards, my dad cautiously asked (as he had so many times before) how I was feeling about my relationship with this man. Usually, this was where the conversation would head south and our lunch would abruptly end with me exploding in anger and retreating to my familiar state of withdrawal in my room. But to his shock and mine, I told him that what had happened between the two of us was wrong and very much worse than what he thought. I began to cry as the words of the story flowed out. I remember falling into my daddy's arms, broken and begging for help. As I opened my heart to let the poisoned lies out, something else much more powerful flowed in—a heavenly Father's love.

I couldn't say exactly what caused the change on that particular day, I only know that the scales had fallen from my eyes. I was finally seeing a tiny glimpse of truth after living so long in deception and lies. After months of defending the very man who had violated me, I agreed to file charges against the perpetrator.

I can only attribute this shift to the power of God working in my life. Supernatural truth had come into my heart and shattered a wall of lies. For the first time I realized that I had been used and tricked. I suddenly felt embarrassed and angry as the reality of the situation sank in, but for once my anger was not fixed on my parents or God but rather on my perpetrator, as well as the real enemy behind it all—the devil himself. This marked the beginning of my travels on the road home.

Depression, Rebellion, and Unhealthy Relationships

One could scarcely imagine the joy and celebration of my family following this day of turning. However, the road home had only just begun, and the extent of the damage to my heart had not yet been discovered. Though one battle had been won, the war for my healing was far from over. Consistency was something that would be unseen in my life for almost two more years. I remember countless places along the journey when I was tempted to give up. Defeated and tired of fighting, I often wondered if true healing was even possible—but I had seen a glimmer of hope, and I chose to press on.

In the early days, the first challenge that I faced was simply getting out of bed. Since I had acknowleged the ugly reality of what had happened, I could no longer live in the fantasy world that I had created. Every day for months I awoke with a fresh reminder of this painful truth, and some days it was simply more than I could bear. I remember times when, after functioning at a reasonable level for a week or two, I just folded up and went back to my room under deep covers of darkness in my bed. These roller coaster days were difficult for those around me. I felt so fragile, like at any moment the small shelter of recovery I had built might shatter, and I would have to begin again.

While this battle raged continually, three dark forces invaded: depression, rebellion, and unhealthy relationships with guys surfaced from somewhere deep inside of me. Each of these dark forces had grown out of the root of sexual abuse. While I can recognize these enemies now, I was clueless back then what I was even fighting against. Because I had experienced this deep trauma during the years of identity formation, I had built my identity around the relationship with the perpetrator. I failed to recognize that this had created a false sense of who I was, so I embraced depression, rebellion, and unhealthy relationships as simply a part of the real me. For a time each of these ugly monsters mastered me, and sometimes all of them at once.

After that first victory in July, these three weaknesses still dominated me. As I struggled simply to function, I used them as coping mechanisms. They were like my crutches to help me make it through days and weeks. Regarding *unhealthy relationships*, I seemed to attract all sorts of dysfunctional boys. I quickly discovered that even in protected Christian environments, I would gravitate toward the most needy and struggling teens in the crowd. I wore an invisible sign advertising my vulnerability and because I felt a desperate need for guys' love and attention, I welcomed any and every advance, even when they were overtly inappropriate and purely lustful.

Regarding *depression*, I struggled with a very hopeless view on life. Despite the fact that I had been on depression medication for several months, a number of my days were still spent in desperate grief, wondering how I could go on.

Regarding *rebellion*, I knew my parents loved me, but I viewed them as power hungry tyrants, intent on ruining my life. Though I believed that I was paving the way for a more free way of life through these expressions of rebelliousness, in reality, every time I used one of them, their dangerous hold on me grew.

From these challenges came other common behaviors and struggles associated with sexual abuse. I became acquainted with self-mutilation, was caught up in many foolish relationships, and developed an eating disorder. Still lacking stability I struggled with a vast array of exaggerated emotions: My view of myself was skewed, so I vacillated from self-hate to vanity. My view of others was skewed, so I vacillated from floating anger to misguided love. My view of God was skewed, so I vacillated from intense rejection to shallow acceptance. Depending on what state I was in at any given time, my level of functioning varied dramatically.

Roller Coaster Recovery

Though struggling on many fronts, I experienced a second explosion of truth that was a milestone on my road home. This second day of turning took place in November of 2003. I had become involved with a wrong crowd of people who were masquerading as Christian teens. I was quickly being pulled down a path of more compromise and sure destruction. After finding myself in a very foolish and dangerous position, I awoke to the truth of what I was doing. The fear of God exploded in my heart, and I began to feel true conviction and a desire for change.

Once again I can only attribute this shift to the awesome power of a merciful God. Almost overnight my outlook on the situation had changed. I began to spend more time with godly people and thus began to be influenced by godliness. I am so thankful for God's timely intervention. Psalm 138:7 says, "Though I walk in the midst of trouble, you preserve my life...with your right hand you save me." God had spared my life again. After this second breakthrough I began to experience more small victories, though the setbacks were still present. Through it all, an anchor of truth had been dropped and it would not fail.

As I began to look to the future, I wondered what I should do with my life. Deep down I really wanted my life to count for something greater than me. Through a series of events that I can only attribute to God, I began to be contacted by Teen Mania Ministries' Honor Academy about a one-year ministry internship they offered for high-school graduates. This program consisted of Bible classes, missions experiences, intense discipleship, and hard work in an assigned department. I really thought nothing much about the periodic calls I received by ministry representatives inviting me to consider interning with the ministry—not, that is, until my parents came to me and expressed that they thought it would be a good option for me after I graduated.

Though not usually one to agree with their ideas, the opportunity to get out of town and do some good for others sounded attractive to me. By the beginning of 2004, I was seriously considering going to the Honor Academy in January of 2005, right after I would graduate high school in December. By doing so I had taken a step toward God, and must have stirred up a lot of spiritual warfare. Suddenly it seemed as if the enemy unleashed all of his best struggles for me, and that whole next year turned into an intense battle for my future.

Throughout 2004, the roller coaster ride of recovery was intensified in my life. At times I functioned quite well for extended periods of time only to take a dramatic crash right into the same rocks that I had visited so many times before: rebellion, anger, rejection, depression, hopelessness, and faulty relationships. I had been on this road of recovery for over a year now and was becoming frustrated that I couldn't reach a place of freedom.

This bad fruit in my life was continuing to grow from the ugly root. The abuse that I had suffered had produced many attitudes, thought patterns, and identities that were foreign to the pure, God-loving girl that I had once been. For weeks or months at a time my parents and I would attempt to attack an area of obvious bondage in my life, only to wind up right where we began time and time again. It wasn't until I was ready and willing to let God's deep healing work into my life that I found much lasting victory.

Despite the struggles I knew progress was being made. Through Joyce Meyer teaching tapes and books, powerful truth was being planted in my heart. But even more significant, God was miraculously paving the way for me to be placed in an environment where He could get through to my heart. Though deeply entangled in a relationship with a young man from our church, warring with my parents on seemingly every decision, struggling to discover who I really was, and fighting to be in charge of my own life, I somehow felt God impress something so strong on my heart that I could not ignore it.

I remember knowing beyond any doubt that I had heard God's voice even in the midst of turmoil, confusion, heartache, and weakness. He told me that if I would step out and go to the Honor Academy, He would sort out and fix everything back home. At the state I was in, this sounded like a pretty good deal. Though I was rejecting most of what God was trying to get through to me at this time, this one promise I grabbed ahold of, and still confused, I reached out with childlike faith.

Unwilling to give up his hold on me, the enemy tried to pull me into erratic, bizarre behaviors to keep me from the destination God had for me. When I say bizarre, I mean bizarre! Like the day that I got mad, threw a golf ball through my window, and used the glass to cut my arms and legs. But God's hand was still at work, preserving my life and leading me on. So after more time of recovery, and despite the intense opposition, I arrived at the Honor Academy in Garden Valley, Texas in 2005. I knew that God had a purpose for my being there, and I settled in, choosing to simply trust. Little did I know that my life was about to be turned upside down.

Final Breakthrough Day

February 11, 2005 is a day I will always treasure as the final breakthrough day. On this ordinary Friday, I encountered the living, holy, all-powerful Creator of the universe, and my life would never be the same again.

The first fasting retreat began five weeks into the Honor Academy. All interns would stop regular activities and fast from Thursday night to Sunday morning with no eating, no talking, nothing at all except seeking the face of Jesus. I was scared. I was still clinging to *my* way of doing things, *my* plans for my future, *my* control of my life. Yet I had a sinking feeling that everything was about to change.

It was the opening ceremony in the auditorium. The lights were dimmed, and worship music filled the room as 600 people cried out to God. Suddenly, it was as if everything ceased. There were no people; there was no music; it was only my heavenly Father and me—my Father that I had rejected, hardened my heart to, and had run from—and this night my Father called me back to Him. I began to utterly break as the Creator of the Universe began to speak clearly to me, revealing the wickedness of my own heart. I felt His presence so strong that I became unaware of my surroundings.

The words God spoke to me were heavy words. They were words of warning and of truth. He showed me that I was a rebel in my heart despite my lip service to my parents and Him. He was giving me a period of grace where I could choose to turn. If I did not change, I would die. I was a prodigal, and it was time to return home. Words cannot describe the severity of God's words that I felt in my heart. I was faced with a choice, yet it did not feel like a choice at all. The power and presence of God were so strong that as soon as I cried out yes, I was literally transformed from the inside out.

I don't know how long I was lying on the hard floor of that auditorium crying out to *my* God. I wept and wailed in realization of my hard heart. I repented and begged God to forgive and cleanse me, and I praised and thanked God for His indescribable mercy in snatching me from the path of death. That night, I reached the end of myself, and the beginning of God's supernatural power of restoration. I had come home to my Father, surrendered to His will for my life, and established Him as *my* Lord.

Throughout the rest of the retreat, God uprooted many of my faulty foundations, cleansed my heart, and set me on the path of life. As I began to see Scripture in truth, it shed light on all of my ways of darkness. Through the book of Proverbs, God showed me that I was the rebel the Scripture talks about, and I was the harlot the Scripture warns about. God also lifted my eyes to the hope of the future He was calling me to—a future of freedom, purpose, and kingdom work. I became excited as I considered the possibilities that my life could hold when it was completely surrendered to Him.

The liberty that I felt was indescribable. The freedom that I had been searching for, fighting for, and begging for was finally mine. I did not find freedom through the doors I expected to find it. Rather, it came through the doors of utter brokenness and radical submission. My life was now open for true restoration and healing.

Immediately when the retreat ended, I took action on what God had done in my heart. Through tears of joy, I called my parents and repented, telling them that I was a prodigal, and I was returning home—home in my heart. I made some other phone calls and wrote some letters too. I had many things to make right. No matter how difficult some of these were, they were all done with new purpose and new joy because I was walking in obedience to the new King and Lord of my life.

After years of shunning authorities and mentors that God had placed in my path, I found myself thanking them—thanking my parents for not letting me ruin my life, thanking my family for loving me when I was unlovable, and thanking countless others for their prayer support during my difficult journey. I had been surrounded with the prayers, love, and support of so many individuals who refused to give up on me, but believed for the breakthrough that had finally come.

This turning point made way for true progress in so many areas of my life. First, my relationship with God became real. I entered into an intimacy with Jesus that I had scarcely imagined possible. As I spent time with the Lord daily, His Word came alive in my heart. A passion for holiness and truth and a desperation for God's presence caused me to dig in to the deep things of God. Second, I became strong enough to truly face the abuse that had happened to me. God used the teachers, mentors, and experiences of the Honor Academy throughout that year to lay a foundation upon which He could rebuild me in His way. Third, God brought restoration within my family. The months and years of hardness, anger, and cruelty toward them had created a large chasm of hurt between me and my parents and siblings. I had a passionate desire to see restoration come in each and every relationship.

I can vividly remember the shock of my family and friends when I came home to visit from Texas. I was not the hardheaded, mean girl who had left just a short time ago. Rather, I was possessed by a fresh love that blossomed out of the true love that had been replanted within the soil of my heart. God's supernatural love had taken me over, and it held the power to restore broken relationships. I had a desire to serve and love my parents and siblings like never before. I realized how much I had taken for granted, and I desperately wanted my place to be restored within the family. They became my support system like they always should have been, but I hadn't allowed them to since the sexual abuse was uncovered. The times that I spent with my family became treasures to me, and I thank God continually for their place in my life.

God had proven Himself victorious—victorious over the enemy's attacks, over pain, and over sin. At the same time, God was preparing me for the continued processes of healing that I would still have to walk through, and the challenges that I would still have to face.

CONCLUSION:

Safe in His Hands!

Kalyn

During my last semester at the Honor Academy, my parents and I found out that two and a half years after filing charges against the man who had abused me, our case was going to trial. Since I was needed in the trial process, I took two weeks of emergency leave from the academy and flew home to testify in court.

Shortly after beginning the process I understood why so few victims of sexual crimes choose to press charges. The gruelling, embarrassing, drawn-out court proceedings were an experience I would wish upon no one. Words cannot express the pain; it was undoubtedly the most difficult thing I have ever had to walk through. I knew that God held my heart, but I still felt afraid. Often during those two weeks I contemplated quitting the process. I sensed the pull of depression and hopelessness knocking at my door, and felt terrified that I was going back to the pit of despair. Yet God's grace was enough, and He pulled all of us through.

The jury found the man guilty of aggravated criminal sexual assault—specifically, indecent solicitation of a minor. I remember the indescribable relief that I felt when the verdict was read and the trial was over. After still struggling with feelings of blame and responsibility over the relationship, it was extremely helpful for my healing to realize that I had been a victim. The abuse that I experienced was not my fault, and the court system had proven this to me.

Though relieved, I felt beaten up by the whole process. Even after I returned to the Honor Academy, I was struggling very much with it. Having to relive all of the events and face the man in court was almost more than I could bear. For several weeks I experienced symptoms of post-traumatic stress disorder, including nightmares, panic attacks, and depression; but through it all the Lord upheld me. Day by day I pressed on, trusting that my God would pull me through.

Ironically, this chapter of my life is not quite closed yet. Through an odd series of events in 2006, the court case was reopened by some new lawyers hired by the defendant, my sexual abuser. After a two-year appeal process in the appellate court, the case was ordered to go to retrial. Now seven years after the events, I could still be subpoenaed to court to testify once again about occurrences from so long ago. I guess I will get to wade through the mess one more time, trusting that God's strength inside of me will be enough to carry me through. Though I don't look forward to reliving those painful memories, I do rejoice in the victory that I know is already mine, for I hope in the One who cannot be defeated!

A Work in Progress

My road home could be described as many things— long, hard, trying, challenging, but also victorious! Now, seven years after I set out on this journey (at the time this book is being written), I can appreciate the joys and struggles along the way, for I can see how God used what the enemy meant for evil in my life and turned it into something good. I now claim Psalm 40:1–3 (NASB) as my life verse.

> I waited patiently for the LORD and He inclined to me and heard my cry. He brought me up out of the pit of destruction, out of the miry clay, and He set my feet upon a rock making my footsteps firm. He put a new song in my mouth, a song of praise to our God; many will see and fear and will trust in the LORD.

God pulled me out of an impossible pit, cleaned me up, and gave me a reason to live! I'm not claiming that my story of restoration is finished. I still find areas of my life that God is healing and restoring just like He promised to do. I can look back through the years and chuckle, realizing sometimes in humorous terms just how far God has brought me. Yet I also recognize with seriousness just how far God still wants to take me.

Some pieces of my healing have taken longer to obtain than others, but I know that God is completing the work that He began in me, and He will not stop until it is finished. I welcome His work in my life, and desire that He form and fashion me just like the potter fashions the clay. (See Isa. 29:16.)

Joining the Front Lines

Sadly, my story is not uncommon. The enemy is picking off young people left and right through the hands of our perverted, godless society. Sexual perversion, abuse, rebellion, depression, suicide, drugs, alcohol, eating disorders, and self-mutilation run rampant in the airwaves. Don't be naive and ignore the symptoms. There is truly a battle raging for the hearts and minds of this present generation. The BattleCry campaign launched by Teen Mania Ministries during the time that I was an intern at the Honor Academy exploded in my heart and continues to impact me in a special way because I have experienced the battle. I have felt the pain of being on the losing side of the war.

Now is the time to rise up and fight and to take your place on the front lines of the battle for your kids, your family, and this generation. I don't know about you, but I am committed to fight for righteousness and truth. I am joining the front lines.

God has put a passion in my heart to carry His message of hope to the world. After graduating from the

Honor Academy in December 2005, I moved back home to be a part of the amazing family that God has given me, and to be involved in the work that He has called our family to do. With my college degree in social work completed, I continue working with our church's REALITY youth ministry. I have a stronger desire than ever to see others experience the hope and joy of Jesus that became real in my life. I have already had so many opportunities to share my story, to tell of God's amazing love, and to live out His work in my life, and I look forward to these times in the future.

I consider it a privilege to serve my King every day, for I will always remember His saving power in my life. I don't know everything that my future holds, but I know that my life will be an agent of hope and a testimony of God's power. The world is full of people who are desperate for a miracle. If my experience helps even one young person, encourages one parent, or gives one family the strength to carry on, than it was worth all the pain. I only desire that God be glorified for His unending love, unwavering faithfulness, and undying power.

On one hand my story is really nothing extraordinary. It is simply one of many accounts of God's absolute faithfulness in the midst of impossible circumstances. On the other hand, my story is something special because what God did for me, He will do for anyone. After walking through the last seven years, I have decided that nothing is impossible with God. No situation is too hopeless, no heart is too hard, and no pain is too deep that our God cannot heal. He is all-powerful and He is able to bring a miracle when one is desperately needed.

So, if you find yourself simply observing the crisis of others or alone in a crisis yourself, sinking in a pit or traveling a road of restoration, I encourage you to press on. Don't quit fighting and don't give up—don't give up on yourself; don't give up on your loved one. Yet more importantly, don't give up on your God! One day you will be on the other side of the story and your eyes will be opened to the greatness, the power, and the mercy of our great God. He is faithful!

One day I stumbled upon John 10:28–29, which says, "I give eternal life to them, and they will never perish; and no one will snatch them out of My hand. My Father, who has given them to Me, is greater than all; and no one is able to snatch them out of the Father's hand" (NASB). As I read those words I suddenly realized that I had *always* been, and always would be, safe in His hands.

Lisa

I look at my bright, articulate, healthy daughter, and my heart swells up with pride. What a champion she is in my book! I've watched her battle back from the brink of destruction to rise up and take her place in the fight to save this young generation.

I look at my Jesus and my heart swells up with pride. How could anyone deny His love and His power when you witness what He did for our family? Never again can I doubt the truth of His covenant. I hope that this book has shown you how much He can be trusted and how faithful He is to keep all His promises.

Writing this book was much harder than I ever imagined it to be. Oh, there were the obstacles that you would logically expect a mother of so many to encounter. I remember sitting in my writing chair one day deep in thought, dressed in half pajamas and half work-out clothes with a one-year-old baby standing on top of a toy truck at my side. He was reaching up to take hold of his favorite security item—my hair. I laughed and wondered what a future publisher would think of my "professional working conditions."

But that's just the point. Kalyn and I are not professional writers. We're just a common Midwestern family with a message to share of God's miracle power. I didn't realize how painful the writing process would be for me—and even more so for Kalyn—

but as we trudged through many writes and re-writes we knew our pain was not without a purpose. Even more importantly, though, we knew that we had to complete our project as a point of obedience to the One who had given us so much.

As God began to open my heart to write this book, He graciously confirmed His words of instruction to me when I was worshipping Him at a Joyce Meyer Ladies Conference. As well-known Christian artist Darlene Zschech was leading us into powerful, intimate worship of our King, she paused in her singing, looked out at the audience, and said, "Ladies, the Lord wants you to know that *you* [and she cupped her hands in front of her] are safe in His hands."

Immediately tears began streaming down my face as the Lord echoed in my own heart, "That word is for you. Your daughter is now and always has been safe in My hands. That's the message of hope I want you to share in your book." So among all the natural, biblical, and personal elements presented here, Kalyn and I have weaved hope into the fabric of this message— hope for God's guidance and direction, for His safety and protection, for miracles and divine intervention; and perhaps best of all, hope for salvation, restoration, and a bright future.

A Dad's Story

An intense personal crisis will put a man to the test. The story you have just read of my family's passage through "the valley of the shadow of death" stretched me almost to the point of breaking. (Ps. 23:4.) A successful family, with godly children, living the great American dream was suddenly thrust toward the rocks of destruction by a tsunami-size wave. What held the ship of my life together was an anchor for my soul. (Heb. 6:19.) That anchor held as the storms ruthlessly beat against our home for over three years.

Prior to October 19, 2002 my faith had not suffered such a test. Through the storm I found that the object of my faith was even more trustworthy than I had believed. How much better I can now relate to the words of Psalm 27:13: "I would have despaired unless I had believed that I would see the goodness of the LORD in the land of the living" (NASB). I know only too well what that feels like. To be in despair is to lose hope. In one of the most poignant chapters of this book (and of our life), Lisa called this "the dark night of the soul."

The best way I could explain a dark night of the soul experience is when life seems so bleak and hopeless, so void of light and so filled with despair, so purposeless and painful that it's nearly unthinkable to go on living. To reach this low point we must be confronted with a crisis that strikes at everything we are, everything we believe, and everything we love.

Lisa wrote in that "dark night" chapter that a mother's dark night is not the same as a father's dark night, and she's right. A mother is the emotional caretaker of the family so when the family is in severe emotional turmoil, Mom's pain is multiplied. But as the God-ordained leader of the family, the father is faced with a "buck stops here" responsibility that is enjoyable when things work, but devastatingly painful when they do not.

When my daughter turned from being a loving and pleasant 15-year-old girl to a self-mutilating, deeply depressed, rebellious runaway, it felt like my legs had been cut out from under me. I was stunned and literally numb. How could I have allowed this to happen on my watch? What did this sudden failure say about my fathering? How could a thief have stolen my daughter from right under my nose? The pain and condemnation tried to sink me into the dark night syndrome.

The total darkness of it all and the speed with which it happened are completely beyond my ability to express with words. "Daddy's girl" seemed to have suddenly been ripped from my hands. She was still there, in some hollow shell of a person, but the girl I had known was gone. Would I ever see her again? In a matter of thirty minutes on that incredible October day, she was morphed into a totally different human being. How could I bear it? In what seemed to be the perfect storm of pain and destruction, it was difficult to see a way out.

Visibility is so much greater on the front or the back of a violent storm. In the midst of the storm, it is difficult to see which way to turn. When you cannot navigate by sight, your only hope is the instrument panel. The Word of God and the leadership of the Holy Spirit miraculously guided Lisa and me through a storm that caught us completely by surprise. One morning, early in the crisis, when guilt, confusion, and torment were gnawing at my inner being, I heard a quiet voice speak to me in my heart, "I will uphold your daughter by the Word of my power." I recognized those words from Hebrews 1:3 (NKJV.) That moment, God laid a foundation stone for me to stand on over the next three years. That stone never gave way.

Here on the other side of the crisis I can see that what Satan meant for evil, God is using for good. My daughter is now a beacon proclaiming the light of Christ that can take young girls through incredible darkness. My wife continues to mother our children with conviction and incredible love while helping other families be restored. My children have experienced God's faithfulness, not just spoken of but personally witnessed in their own home. And Dad...well I have been changed to the core.

An experience that could have broken me revealed some things in my life that *needed* to be broken: pride, self-trust, independence. I still dimly remember hearing the voice of the accuser during our most desperate times of pain, darkness, and despair: "She will never come out of it. You are a failure. Your family is a farce." I am so grateful to God that through the whole process and as we proceed toward the future, we were, are, and always will be safe in His hands.

Why You Should Read the Tools and Resources

Whole volumes have been written and are worth perusing on the subject of adolescence. I have a personal theory as to why those adolescent parenting books sell well: the average parent has run into an adolescent parenting brick wall—and then decided to go for help. I have to confess that most of my teen parenting book purchases occurred after October 19, 2002—not before. Maybe you are reading this book today because you've hit a parenting brick wall. Even if you are still sailing in calm parenting waters, I hope that our story and these Tools and Resources will encourage you to practice a little preventive maintenance and avoid the teen crisis storm in the first place.

Some of my best finds of resources were unusual picks for me, such as *Yes, Your Teen Is Crazy!—Loving Your Kid Without Losing Your Mind* by secular psychologist Dr. Michael Bradley. His book is often crude and ungodly in language and not the kind of book to leave around on your coffee table. Yet it was an important vehicle that God used to help me understand the interesting and controversial new research about the adolescent brain. For instance, Dr. Bradley wrote,

"The old thinking that the brain game is over by age five is wrong. The most critical years for your young adolescent are likely yet to be. The good and bad news is that, first, this wild brain development may create new, unpredictable thought pathways, wherein action thoughts can outrace judgment capabilities just as they did in early childhood...Remember 12 years ago when your teen was a toddler and you walked in to find him sitting in the cat box munching on some scary litter? Remember last week when your teen used the pressure washer to clean your car, stripping off about $500 worth of paint before she realized this was not such a good idea? Do the words *impulsive* and *poor judgment* come to mind? Can you draw that 2-year-old face onto that 12-year-old body? Learn this trick well, because we're going to use it a lot. Both that toddler and adolescent brain at times are unstable, dysfunctional, and completely unpredictable.[1]

That one technique was worth my purchase of his book. I can draw that 2-year-old face with the best of them now—and have greater understanding of my spewing adolescent in the process.

While some may question the accuracy of Dr. Bradley's scientific findings about adolescent brain development, his writings accurately portray many teenage struggles. Yet it would be unfair to portray all teens through the lens of his research, for while adolescent craziness is a real possibility for a teen who is walking in the flesh (led by the impulses of mind and emotions) not all teens are hopelessly walking in the flesh.

Pastor Paul David Tripp is highly effective at pointing us to another view of adolescence in his book, *Age of Opportunity—A Biblical Guide to Parenting Teens*:

"It is time for us to reject the wholesale cynicism of our culture regarding adolescence. Rather than years of undirected and unproductive struggle, these are years of unprecedented opportunity. They are the golden age of parenting, when you begin to reap all the seeds you have sown in their lives, when you can help your teenager to internalize truth preparing him or her for a productive, God-honoring life as an adult. These are the years of penetrating questions...of wonderful discussions never before possible...of failure and struggle that put the teen's true heart on the table...of daily ministry and of great opportunity. These are not the years merely to be survived! They are to be approached with a sense of hope and a sense of mission."[2]

These authors may seem to be in conflict of views— one sees teen problems and another teen potential—but I believe they're both right. I have watched our own teenagers and many others spiral off into fleshly, outlandish craziness one minute and then rise up with surprising spiritual maturity the next. I have witnessed firsthand the power of God moving in a group of teens and drawing them upward to incredible levels of leadership to their peers. Then I have witnessed disaster hit one of those same precious teens the next week and cause him or her to appear trapped in crazy thinking. That's what tends to keep us parents humble and on our knees for direction and answers!

Parents must be willing to dig inside the twenty-first century teen world and strive to understand our inner struggles. Remember, we have a generation in crisis! It is not just us "spiritual" writers who are saying such a thing. Dr. Bradley says:

> "Our research shows adolescent personality to be amazingly similar over time.... So if kids are essentially the same as we were, why do they seem so particularly crazy these days? Two reasons.
>
> "The first reason is....we've somehow come to view adolescents as if they were adults and not children. From the kid's perspective, this wish is nothing new. Teenagers of all generations have lobbied for adult privileges with the swaggering assurances that they can handle 'it.' The fact is that they cannot handle 'it' *and they know this.* They cannot handle the dangerous pressures confronting them without some structure from their parents, yet they'll go to war over imposed parental structure... adolescents today are powerful because we've

allowed them to become that way, stupid because their brain-challenged, and seriously at-risk because...the world we've created around them is truly insane."[3]

Which brings me to the main reason for this section— I implore you to do your own research and draw your own conclusions. I have provided many tools and resources here (as well as throughout the book) for you to look into and to help you learn all you can about your teenager and what to do during this Journey through adolescence.

You must understand your parental charge from God. *You* are going to have to lead that sweet, struggling son or daughter of yours through the passage from childhood to adulthood—and the only way to successfully make it through this Journey with them is to be equipped with the right tools and information.

TOOL 1

Lisa's Scripture Confession

Speaking scriptures aloud regularly is how we get the power of God's Word working in our situation. (Rom. 10:17.) And it can cause faith to supernaturally rise up in our spirit and before long we realize that we're believing the Word. So I'm sharing my confessions I spoke (and still speak) during our parenting crisis with Kalyn. Through that, more than anything in life so far, I have found God to be faithful to His Word.

I encourage you to add to this list by asking the Lord to guide you to scriptures that are specific for you and your situations. Then take His Word, personalize it for you and your loved ones, and begin to pray it out loud. God has promised that His Word won't and can't return void but will accomplish that for which it was sent. (Isa. 55:11.)

My Mind:

Colossians 3:1-17
Since, then, I have been raised with Christ, I set my heart on things above, where Christ is seated at the right hand of God. I set my mind on things above, not on earthly things. For I died, and my life is now hidden with Christ in God. When

Christ, who is my life, appears, then I also will appear with him in glory.

I put to death, therefore, whatever belongs to my earthly nature: sexual immorality, impurity, lust, evil desires and greed, which is idolatry. Because of these, the wrath of God is coming. I used to walk in these ways, in the life I once lived. But now I must rid myself of all such things as these: anger, rage, malice, slander, and filthy language from my lips. I will not lie to others, since I have taken off the old self with its practices and have put on the new self, which is being renewed in knowledge in the image of its Creator. Here there is no Greek or Jew, circumcised or uncircumcised, barbarian, Scythian, slave or free, but Christ is all, and is in all.

Therefore, as God's chosen people, holy and dearly loved, I clothe myself with compassion, kindness, humility, gentleness, and patience. I bear with others and forgive whatever grievances I have against another. I forgive as the Lord forgave me. And over all these virtues I put on love, which binds them all together in perfect unity.

I let the peace of Christ rule in my heart, since as members of one body I was called to peace. And I am thankful. I let the word of Christ dwell in me richly as I teach and admonish others with all wisdom, and as I sing psalms, hymns and spiritual songs with gratitude in my heart to God. And whatever I do, whether in word or deed, I do it all in the name of the Lord Jesus, giving thanks to God the Father through him.

I put your covenant of increase on my mind.

My Eyes:

Like Job, I've made a covenant with my eyes:
I ask you:

Open my eyes that I may see wonderful things in your law. (Ps 119:18)

I lift up my eyes to the hills where does my help come from? My help comes from the Lord, the Maker of heaven and earth. (Ps 121:1)

But my eyes are fixed on you, sovereign Lord. (Ps 141:8)

I fix my eyes on Jesus, the author and perfecter of my faith. (Heb 12:2)

I fix my eyes not on what is seen but on what is unseen. (2 Cor 4:18)

I choose to walk by faith and not by sight. (2 Cor 5:7)

I will not be wise in my own eyes. I fear the Lord and shun evil. (Pro 3:7)

I open my eyes and look at the fields! They are ripe as to harvest. (John 4:35)

I will set before my eyes no worthless thing. I hate the work of those who fall away. (Ps 101:3)

My Ears:

I am quick to listen, slow to speak and slow to become angry. (James 1:9)

I am a wise woman for I listen to advice. (Pro 12:15)

I am Jesus' sheep, and I listen to his voice; the voice of a stranger I simply do not listen to. (John 10:27)

Speak Lord for your servant is listening. (1 Sam 3:9)

My Mouth:

You've put a new song in my mouth, a hymn of praise to my God. (Ps 40:3)

His praise will always be on my lips. (Ps 34:1)

May my lips overflow with praise. (Ps 119:171)

I will put a muzzle on my mouth, and I will keep my tongue from sin. (Ps 39:1)

I will not let this book of the law depart from my mouth. (Joshua 1:8)

I keep my lips from speaking lies. (Ps 34:13)

I keep a tight rein on my tongue. (James 1:26)

The Lord is my help for no man can tame the tongue. (James 3:8)

I have wisdom, she is my sister and the tongue of the wise brings healing. (Pro 12:18)

I only speak that which is good to edifying. (Eph 4:29)

Psalm 91

I dwell in the shelter of the Most High and I will rest in the shadow of the Almighty

I will say of the LORD, "He is my refuge and my fortress, my God, in whom I trust."

Surely he will save me from the fowler's snare and from the deadly pestilence.

He will cover me with his feathers, and under his wings I will find refuge;

His faithfulness will be my shield and rampart.

I will not fear the terror of night, nor the arrow that flies by day,

Nor the pestilence that stalks in the darkness, nor the plague that destroys at midday.

A thousand may fall at my side, ten thousand at my right hand,

But it will not come near me.

I will only observe with my eyes and see the punishment of the wicked.

If I make the Most High my dwelling—even the LORD, who is my refuge

Then no harm will befall me, no disaster will come near my tent.

For he will command his angels concerning me to guard me in all my ways;

They will lift me up in their hands, so that I will not strike my foot against a stone.

I will tread upon the lion and the cobra; I will trample the
    great lion and the serpent.
Because I love the Lord, he says he will rescue me;
He will protect me, for I acknowledge his name.
I will call upon him, and he will answer me;
He will be with me in trouble, he will deliver me and
    honor me.
With long life he will satisfy me and show me his salvation."

My words are aptly spoken like apples of gold
in settings of silver. (Pr 25:11)

My No'se:

Whatever you bind on earth will be bound in heaven. (Matt
16:19) I say no to:
(List whatever the Lord puts on your heart for you and
your family's situation. Add as needed.)

Sin
Worry
Fear
Terror
Devil
Rebellion
Sickness and Disease
Accidents
Poverty
Mental Torment
Oppression
Depression
Unproductivity
Confusion
Idolatry
Pride
Self-will
Lust
Bondage

Wrong Dating Relationships
Wrong Friendships
Gluttony
Eating Disorders
Food Addictions
Poor Self Image
Roots of Rejection
Sibling Rivalry
Slothfulness
Laziness
Disorderliness
Intimidation
Man-Pleasing
Contemplation
Condemnation
Strife
Doubt
Unbelief
Immodest Dress
Selfishness
Overspending
Marital Conflict
Nagging

I say "yes" to the blessings over my family.

Deuteronomy 28 says:

If we fully obey the LORD our God and carefully follow all his commands we are given today, the LORD our God will set us high above all the nations on earth. All these blessings will come upon us and accompany us if we obey the LORD our God:

We will be blessed in the city and blessed in the country.

The fruit of our womb will be blessed, and the crops of our land and the young of our livestock—the calves of our herds and the lambs of our flocks.

Our basket and our kneading trough will be blessed.

We will be blessed when we come in and blessed when we go out.

The LORD will grant that the enemies who rise up against us will be defeated before us. They will come at us from one direction but flee from us in seven.

The LORD will send a blessing on our barns and on everything we put our hands to. The LORD our God will bless us in the land he is giving us.

The LORD will establish us as his holy people, as he promised us on oath, if we keep the commands of the LORD our God and walk in his ways. Then all the peoples on earth will see that we are called by the name of the LORD, and they will fear us. The LORD will grant us abundant prosperity—in the fruit of our womb, the young of our livestock and the crops of our ground—in the land he swore to our forefathers to give us.

The LORD will open the heavens, the storehouse of his bounty, to send rain on our land in season and to bless all the work of our hands. We will lend to many nations but will borrow from none. The LORD will make us the head, not the tail. If we pay attention to the commands of the LORD our God that He gives us this day and carefully follow them, we will always be at the top, never at the bottom. We do not turn aside from any of the commands he gives us today, to the right or the left, following other gods and serving them.

I abide in the vine!

My Heart:

I have no fear of bad news, my heart is steadfast. (Psalm 112:7)

I watch over my heart with all diligence for from it flows
the springs of life. (Pro 4:23)

I love the Lord my God with all my heart, soul, and mind.
(Matt 22:37)

I fix these words of yours in my heart. (Deut 11:18)

I do not harden my heart. (Heb 3:8)

Search me, O God, and know my heart. (Ps 139:23)

Create in me a pure heart, O God, and renew a right spirit.
(Ps 51:10)

A broken and contrite heart you will not despise. (Ps 51)

Give me Lord an undivided heart. (Ps 86:11)

May the meditation of my heart be pleasing to you.
(Ps 19:14)

I thank you Lord that you are greater than my heart.
(1 John 3:20)

I pour out my heart to you. (Ps 62:8)

I do not let my heart be troubled. (John 14:1)

I have set my heart on pilgrimage. (Ps 86)

A cheerful heart is good medicine—I stir up the joy. (Ps 17:22)

Thank you that you heal the broken hearted and bind up
my wounds. (Ps 147:3)

My Hands:

Who may ascend your holy hill, he who has <u>clean hands</u>
and a pure heart. (Ps 24:4)

I lift up holy hands in prayer. (1 Tim 2:8)

My times are in your hands, O God. (Ps 31:15)

I do not fear for you uphold me by your righteous right
hand. (Isaiah 41:10)

I have laid my hands to the plow, I do not look back.
(Luke 9:62)

Ephesians 6:13-17

Therefore I put on the full armor of God, so that when the day of evil comes, I may be able to stand my ground, and after I have done everything, to stand. I stand firm then, with the belt of truth buckled around my waist, with the breastplate of righteousness in place, and with my feet fitted with the readiness that comes from the gospel of peace. In addition to all this, I take up the shield of faith, with which I can extinguish all the flaming arrows of the evil one. I take the helmet of salvation and the sword of the Spirit, which is the word of God. And I pray in the Spirit on all occasions with all kinds of prayers and requests. With this in mind, I am alert and always keep on praying for all the saints.

My Feet:

You've set my feet upon a rock. (Ps 40:2)

Your word is a lamp to my feet. (Ps 119:105)

How beautiful are my feet for I am bringing good news. (Rom 10:15)

I am going into all the world preaching the good news, making disciples of all nations baptizing them in the name of the Father, Son, and Holy Spirit. (Matt 28:19)

Like Joshua, every place the soles of my feet tread belongs to me. (Joshua 1:3)

I'm taking dominion and authority to trample on snakes and scorpions and over all the power of the enemy. (Luke 10:19)

I do not let the sun go down on my anger, and I do not give the devil a foothold. (Eph 4:27)

My feet are shod with the preparation of the gospel of peace. (Eph 6:14)

I'm taking the path of righteousness, following the blood of the martyrs

I overcome by the blood of the lamb, word of my testimony, and I love not my own life even unto death. (Rev 12:11)

AMEN.

TOOL 2

Understanding Sexual Abuse

I have included some of my favorite excerpts from resources that I have found helpful in recognizing and understanding widespread problems of sexual abuse. Commonly quoted in the literature is an estimation that 1-in-6 to 1-in-4 girls and about 1-in-6 boys will be sexually abused by age 18. Since many occurrences go unreported, accurate statistics are a challenge, but obviously *all parents* need to be educated about this danger! I encourage you to do more research beyond the scope of these excerpts.

From *Identifying Child Molesters: Preventing Child Sexual Abuse by Recognizing the Patterns of the Offenders* by Carla van Dam, PhD:

"Molesters typically sexually abuse children only after they have first charmed adults into believing they are above reproach. This is a premeditated approach hundreds of molesters describe using. Only after the adults have embraced them with wild enthusiasm do they begin to molest the children. This book identifies the predatory pattern and provides the tools to prevent its occurrence. If it were easy to stop molesters, this book would not be needed. Their unbelievably winning ways handily turn the adult community into convert allies in the seduction of children. In case after case, adults become incredibly charmed by someone whose behavior should be worrisome. Instead of alarm, they respond to that charm like deer caught in the headlights of a car, not only failing to protect children, but subsequently, also vociferously defending the molester when allegations do arise.

"Current child sexual abuse prevention strategies are primarily geared toward stopping abuse from continuing after it has already begun. This kind of prevention requires children to be in charge of their own protection. They are taught about 'good touch/bad touch' told to say 'no' to those who try to harm them, asked to relay this information to trusted adults, and instructed to keep telling until they are believed. Rather than relying on children to be the principal line of defense, it is time for adults to take over the job of protecting children by no longer giving molesters access to them."[1]

From *The Wounded Heart: Hope for Adult Victims of Childhood Sexual Abuse* by Dr. Dan B. Allender.[2]

Types of Sexual Abuse: Contact and Interaction

Contact
Very Severe: Genital Intercourse (forcible or nonforcible); oral or anal sex (forcible or nonforcible)

Severe: Unclothed genital contact, including manual touching or penetration (forcible or nonforcible); unclothed breast contact (forcible or nonforcible); simulated intercourse

Least Severe: Sexual kissing (forcible or nonforcible); sexual touching of buttocks, thighs, legs, or clothed breasts or genitals

Interactions
Verbal: Direct solicitation for sexual purposes; seduction (subtle) solicitation or innuendo; description of sexual practices; repeated use of sexual language and sexual terms as personal names

Visual: Exposure to or use for pornography; intentional (repeated) exposure to sexual acts, sexual organs, and/or sexually provocative attire (bra, nighties, slip, underwear); inappropriate attention (scrutiny) directed toward body (clothed or unclothed) or clothing for purpose of sexual stimulation

Psychological: Physical/sexual boundary violation: Intrusive interest in menstruation, clothing, pubic development; repeated use of enemas

Sexual/relational boundary violation: Intrusive interest in child's sexual activity, use of child as a spouse surrogate (confidant, intimate companion, protector, or counselor)

Grooming Behaviors

An excellent synopsis of this is the online source www.texaspolicecentral.com:

"Offenders spend a great deal of time and energy in the process of grooming the child. They generally gain the child's trust and confidence to begin the process. Because the offender is generally someone known to the child, the child may feel that he/she has no alternative but to accept the abuse.

"The next step is to introduce the child to sexual types of touch. This is often accomplished slowly, so that the child is gradually desensitized to the touch.

"Sexual offenders then manipulate the child to keep the secret. The offender may trick or force a child into keeping the sexual abuse a secret by using subtle tactics, such as:

- Bribery—'I'll let you watch TV late if you let me do this.'
- Threats of Harm to the Child—'You are really going to get it if you tell anyone.'
- Threats of Harm to the Offender—'If you tell, I'll go to jail.'
- Break-Up of the Family—'This would really hurt your mother if she knew.'"[3]

Facts That Challenge Misconceptions About Child Sexual Abuse and Child Molesters

From *When Your Child Has Been Molested: A Parent's Guide to Healing and Recovery*

✗ Children do not seduce adults.

✗ Child molesters represent all age, economic, ethnic, social, racial, and religious groups. They can be geniuses, of normal intelligence, or intellectually slow.

✗ Child molesters are single, married, divorced, or separated. They are heterosexual, bisexual, or homosexual. And they can be male or female.

✗ The majority of people who sexually abuse children know their victims.

✗ Many sex offenders do not molest only one time. And they may have molested one or a number of children several times.

✗ Sexual molestation can be as devastating for teenagers as it is for younger children.

✗ The same attention should be paid to very young children as well as older youth when seeking help for their sexual abuse.

✗ Children and youth who are molested usually experience a freezing response within their bodies that can inhibit their ability to fight or resist their molesters. It's unrealistic to expect kids to speak out or fight when they are in this circumstance, although some children do.

✗ Children can molest other children. Although the intervention that occurs with them is different from that of adult child molesters, their behavior should be disrupted and at the very least clarified with a sexual abuse investigation worker.

✗ A growing number of women are being prosecuted for child sexual assault.

✗ Many child molesters were molested themselves as children, but the vast majority of molested children do not grow up to be child sex offenders.[5]

Recognizing Signs and Symptoms of Abuse (in toddlers through teenage children)

From *Beyond the Darkness: Healing for Victims of Sexual Abuse* by Cynthia A. Kubetin and James Mallory, M.D.

1. Nightmares

2. Withdrawal

3. Pseudo-maturity

4. Violent play

5. Low self-esteem

6. Fear of undressing

7. Stomach pain/headaches

8. Running away from home

9. Outbursts of anger

10. Early sexual promiscuity

11. Fear of being alone

12. Unprovoked crying spells

13. Sexually transmitted disease

14. Pregnancy or fear of pregnancy

15. Clinging to significant adult

16. Excessive bathing or brushing of teeth

17. Loss of appetite/increase in appetite

18. Refusal to go to school/leaving school

19. Fear of specific person(s), situation(s), or stranger(s)

20. Vaginal discharge/unusual odor in genital area

21. Seductive or sexual behavior with peers or adults

22. Bleeding, bruises, or problems walking or sitting

23. Pain, itching, redness on genitalia, vaginal, and anal area

24. Increase in activity level/decrease in attention span

25. Behavior problems at school/change in school performance[6]

Differentiating Adolescent Sexual Abuse

From *We are Not Alone: A Guidebook for Helping Professional and Parents Supporting Adolescent Victims of Sexual Abuse* by Jade Christine Angelica, Mdiv:

"In spite of the speculation that the number of sexual abuse reports made by adolescent victims is the tip of the iceberg of actual incidents, a review of the statistics will reveal that *preteens and teenagers comprise the largest percentage of reported sexual abuse victims...* Professionals believe this wider discrepancy may be due to the way society views risks to young children and risks to adolescents. As children mature, the general public perceives the risks of abuse to diminish. Due to their growing physical stature and maturing cognitive ability to reason, adolescents are often seen as having more options to fight, run away to protect themselves in other ways from sexual abuse. If, in fact, a sexual encounter did occur between an adolescent and an adult, society could perceive that a sexually developing adolescent asked for it, initiated it (Gil, 1996), or consented to it since he or she did not choose to fight or run away or find other forms of protection.[7]

Adolescent Specific Symptoms of Sexual Abuse

"Many studies have been done to identify reactions to child sexual abuse, and the list of the most common reactions displayed by adolescent victims is alarmingly long and complex. Adolescent reactions include: alienation from school and peers, anger, anxiety, denial, depression, dissociation, drug and alcohol abuse or addiction, eating disorders, fear, feeling defective, guilt and shame regarding the abuse, hyperarousal, inability to trust, insomnia, low self-esteem, lying and manipulating to gain power and control over others, negative self-perception, panic attacks, school problems, self-mutilation, sexual promiscuity, suicide ideation or attempts, and vulnerability to stress (Briere and Elliott, 1994; Deblinger and Heflin, 1996; Elliott and Briere, 1992; Friedrich, 1995; Gil, 1996, cites Bagley, 1995; Lee, 1995). Often adolescent victims try to communicate about the abuse they have endured through acting-out behavior instead of words. *Unfortunately, observers and recipients of these behaviors, viewing them through the stereotypical lens of 'difficult adolescent,' could mistakenly interpret these cries for help as abuse of others, carelessness, or rebellion.*"[8]

For Help with Child Abuse Prevention for Your Family

Helpful Web sites:

1. Darkness2light.org—Excellent help for prevention programs and help for abuse victims.

2. www.StopItNow.org—Child sexual abuse prevention for parents, caregivers and professionals who work with families and children.

3. www.childpredators.com—Reports on the shocking statistics of underage girls impregnated by adult men and then coerced into abortion.

4. www.missingkids.com—Web site for the National Center for Missing and Exploited Children. Their resources greatly assist law enforcement and legal professionals as well as child care providers and parents.

TOOL 3

Recognizing Adolescent Depression

From the online source www.nlm.nih.gov:

"True depression in teens is often *difficult to diagnose* because normal adolescents have both up and down moods. These moods may alternate over a period of hours or days.

"Adolescent girls are twice as likely as boys to experience depression.

"Symptoms:

- Acting-out behavior (missing curfews, unusual defiance)
- Appetite changes (usually a loss of appetite but sometimes an increase)
- Criminal behavior (such as shoplifting)
- Depressed or irritable mood
- Difficulty concentrating
- Difficulty making decisions
- Episodes of memory loss
- Excessive sleeping or daytime sleepiness

- Excessively irresponsible behavior pattern
- Excessive or inappropriate feelings of guilt
- Failing relations with family and friends
- Faltering school performance
- Fatigue
- Feelings of worthlessness, sadness, or self-hatred
- Loss of interest in activities
- Persistent difficulty falling asleep or staying asleep (insomnia)
- Plans to commit suicide or actual suicide attempt
- Preoccupation with self
- Reduced pleasure in daily activities
- Substance abuse
- Temper (agitation)
- Thoughts about suicide or obsessive fears or worries about death
- Weight change (unintentional weight loss or gain)

"If these symptoms persist for at least 2 weeks and cause significant distress or difficulty functioning, get treatment."[1]

TOOL 4

Suicide Alertness

From the online source www.teensuicide.us:

"It is important to take the warning signs of teen suicide seriously and to seek help if you think that you know a teenager who might be suicidal. Here are some of the things to look for:

- Disinterest in favorite extracurricular activities
- Problems at work and losing interest in a job
- Substance abuse, including alcohol and drug (illegal and legal drugs) use
- Behavioral problems
- Withdrawing from family and friends
- Sleep changes
- Changes in eating habits
- Begins to neglect hygiene and other matters of personal appearance
- Emotional distress brings on physical complaints (aches, fatigues, migraines)
- Hard time concentrating and paying attention

- Declining grades in school
- Loss of interest in schoolwork
- Risk taking behaviors
- Complains more frequently of boredom
- Does not respond as before to praise

"Not all of these teen suicide warning signs will be present in cases of possible teen suicide. There are many cases in which a good student commits suicide. It is important to watch for two or three signs as indications of depression, or even teen suicidal thoughts.

"Understanding that teen suicide warning signs are serious calls for help is important. Many teenagers share their thoughts and feelings in a desperate attempt to be acknowledged. In many cases, they don't know how to deal with their feelings and problems and are looking for someone to help them find assistance. Acknowledging these warning signs and seeking help for the problem, and offering support to a teenager who is working through his or her issues is very important, and can help prevent suicide. Teen suicide is a very real danger, and heeding the warning signs can truly save a life."[1]

(For more information about suicide plans, please see www.teensuicide.us.)

TOOL 5

Differentiating Normal from Abnormal Teenage Rebellion

From *Spiritual Warfare and Your Children: When Your Child Is Under Attack and What to Do About It* by Ray Beeson and Kathi Mills[1]:

(For each normal rebellion there is a corresponding abnormal rebellion.)

Normal

1. Your child wants his or her curfew extended to that of his or her friends.

2. Your child exhibits mood swings but is not violent or destructive.

3. Your child shows less interest in family activities.

4. Your child shows some impatience with family rules and restrictions.

5. Your child asks for what, at times, seems an excessive amount of money for personal expenses.

6. Your child's interests, activities, and/or friends show a gradual change.

7. Your child has an occasional difficulty at school.

8. You child doesn't confide in you as often as before.

9. Your child asks to dress in a popular style of which you do not approve.

10. Your child shows an interest in music or movies of which you do not approve.

Abnormal

1. Your child ignores curfew, sometimes staying out all night.

2. You child's mood swings are becoming more and more irrational and violent.

3. Your child has withdrawn from the family entirely, except for using the home as a "bed and breakfast."

4. Your child not only disobeys you but also speaks disrespectfully to you, even verbally abusing you.

5. You child steals money from you.

6. Your child drops all former interests, activities, and/ or friends.

7. Your child's grades, school behavior, and attendance drop suddenly.

8. Your child becomes sneaky and secretive, even dishonest and manipulative.

9. Your child dresses in such a way that he or she knows will shock and offend you.

10. Your child defiantly listens to music with offensive lyrics, playing it as loudly as possible.

Note (Lisa): *While we are not in any way insinuating that all teens must exhibit rebellion to be normal, we do acknowledge that it's a common temptation for them to struggle with it during the process of teenage individuation and movement toward independence. Learning to recognize and support our kids in their temptation is so important. Learning to recognize the spiritual stronghold of pathological rebellion is essential.*

TOOL 6

Warning Signs and Symptoms of Eating Disorders

From Focus on the Family's Web site (www.troubledwith.com):

Are there signs/symptoms of eating disorders?

"Early detection of an eating disorder may prevent a teenager from years of significant misery and disruption in his or her life. Take a moment and think about your teenager's behavior and [these] signs of a possible eating disorder:

- Preoccupation with weight, food, calories, and dieting
- Exercise is an excessive, rigid activity despite fatigue, illness, injury or weather
- Constant complaints about being fat in spite of normal or thin appearance
- Frequent comparison of body image/diet with others
- Unnatural facial hair growth in girls due to malnutrition
- Withdrawal from activities because of weight and shape concerns

- Anxiety about being fat which does not diminish with weight loss
- Evidence of self-induced vomiting
- Messes and smells in the bathroom
- Disappearing to the bathroom after meals
- Swelling of the glands near the ear which creates a 'chipmunk' appearance (caused by inflammation of the saliva glands)
- Evidence (wrappers, coupons, advertisements, etc.) of the use of laxatives, diuretics, diet pills, enemas
- Consumption of large amounts of food inconsistent with the person's weight, or hoarding/stealing food
- Alternating periods of restrictive dieting and overeating sometimes accompanied by dramatic weight gain or loss
- Cessation or erratic menstrual cycles
- Obsession with appearance as a definition of self which is often accompanied by perfectionist thinking
- Fainting, lightheadedness or dizziness not explained by any other medical problem
- Unusual redness and puffiness around the eyes caused by purging, binge eating and overeating
- Poor dental hygiene, bad breath, dryness of the mouth area and cracked lips caused by purging and dehydration
- Abnormal sleeping patterns
- Hyperactivity
- Refusal to eat meals with family
- Food rituals (such as eating food in rigid sequence, foods cannot touch each other, eating a very limited variety of foods, cutting food into small pieces, blotting foods with napkins to remove fat)"[1]

TOOL 7

Warning Signs of Teenage Drug Abuse

From parentingteens.about.com:

"Please note that even though some of these warning signs of drug abuse may be present in your teen, it does not mean that they are definitely abusing drugs. There are other causes for some of these behaviors. Even the life stage of adolescence is a valid reason for many of them to exist.

"On the flip side of that, do not ignore the warning signs of teenage drug abuse. If six of these signs (not all in the same category) are present for a period of time, you should talk to your teen and seek some professional help [these are partial lists].

Signs in the Home

- Loss of interest in family activities
- Disrespect for family rules
- Withdrawal from responsibilities
- Verbally or physically abusive
- Sudden increase or decrease in appetite

- Disappearance of valuable items or money
- Not coming home on time
- Not telling you where they are going
- Constant excuses for behavior
- Spending a lot of time in their rooms
- Lies about activities
- Finding the following: cigarette rolling papers, pipes, roach clips, small glass vials, plastic baggies, remnants of drugs (seeds, etc.)

Signs at School

- Sudden drop in grades
- Truancy
- Loss of interest in learning
- Sleeping in class
- Poor work performance
- Not doing homework
- Defiant of authority
- Poor attitude towards sports or other extracurricular activities
- Reduced memory and attention span
- Not informing you of teacher meetings, open houses, etc.

Physical and Emotional Signs

- Changes friends
- Smell of alcohol or marijuana on breath or body
- Unexplainable mood swings an behavior

- Negative, argumentative, paranoid or confused, destructive, anxious
- Over-reacts to criticism/acts rebellious
- Sharing few if any of their personal problems
- Doesn't seem as happy as they used to be
- Overly tired or hyperactive
- Drastic weight loss or gain
- Unhappy and depressed
- Cheats, steals
- Always needs money, or has excessive amounts of money
- Sloppiness in appearance"[1]

TOOL 8

Online Safety

Because the technology and trends of Internet usage change so frequently, we recommend you keep updated using an excellent Web site provided by the National Center for Missing and Exploited Children. They can answer specific questions such as, "What should I do if my child is talking to a predator online?"

Go to: www.netsmartz411.org

Other helpful Web sites:

- www.kalynssecret.org—We have included statistics and studies on pornography and online issues.
- www.nationalcoalition.org
- www.filterreview.com
- www.cybertipline.com or 1-800-843-5678
- www.safefamilies.org

TOOL 9

Signs and Symptoms of Cutting

From *Cut: Mercy for Self-Harm* by Nancy Alcorn:

"You may be thinking, *I know someone who does that* or *I do that, but it's really not a big deal.* However, if you are inflicting any self-harming behavior on yourself, it *is* a big deal.

"Self-harm is the outward expression of pain and hurt deep within. Some of the signs and symptoms of self-harming behavior look like this:

- Inflicting cuts with any type of sharp object, usually on an area of the body not normally exposed
- Constant scratching as a response to pressure or unexpected circumstances
- Picking at scabs and preventing the healing process from taking place
- Burning the skin on a regular basis with erasers, fire, or small heat-conducting appliances or metals
- Punching the body, including beating the head against walls or other inanimate objects
- Biting the inside of the mouth or the skin of the arms, hands, or legs

- Pulling hair out—including eyelashes and eyebrows
- Breaking bones or severely bruising the body

"Girls minimize self-harm by saying things such as 'I only pick at my skin sometimes when I am emotional' or 'Well, at least I don't really hurt myself, like break my leg or something, It's just a cut here and there. It's just a nervous habit.' But the truth is: if you are cutting, burning, bruising, biting, chewing, scratching, or purposefully harming yourself in any way, you are struggling with self-harm…

"Girls who self-harm often do it to communicate feelings and emotions they don't know how to verbalize. Anxiety, fear, loneliness, nervousness, and anger are some of the destructive emotions girls try to deal with by choosing to self-injure."[1]

RESOURCES

1. Recommended Reading List for Parents and Teens

I love to read, and I am so grateful that God brings revelations to me through the writings of the body of Christ. I feel that, as believers, we should always be growing and changing. I know as a mother and wife that I still need so much more wisdom! So this is one of my favorite sections of our book as we are honored to recommend the many resources and ministries that God is using to disciple our family.

Remember the principles we have learned as you consider these resources. In order to receive our battle plans from the Lord, we must be willing to do some unusual things—like receiving wisdom and revelation from sources we would not naturally be inclined to consult. We have learned that God does not seem to grace any one person, one book, one denomination, or one ministry with all of His wisdom. We truly do need each other to stay properly balanced. (Rom. 12:21.)

As God has stretched us, we have discovered He is a God of radical balances. Sometimes we need to study radical faith (promises, miracles, and gifts) and sometimes we need to study radical discipleship (brokenness, humility, and discipline). Both sides of the balance are of Him. I encourage you to allow the Holy Spirit to be your Guide, Mentor, and Teacher as you sift through these teachings.

Kalyn and I share our personal thoughts about these resources on our Web site www.Kalynssecret.org. We will continue to update our recommendations there as new resources come to our attention.

Building (or Rebuilding) the Parent/Child Relationship

Bradley, Reb. *Child Training Tips: What I Wish I Knew When My Children Were Young.* Farr Oaks, CA: Family Ministries Publishers, 1998.

Campbell, Ross. *How to Really Love Your Angry Child.* Colorado Springs: David C. Cook, 2004.

Davis, Dr. S. M. *How to Win the Heart of a Rebel.* Oak Brook, IL: IBLP, CD format; available from http://store.iblp.org/products/CWHR/.

Luce, Ron. *ReCreate: Building a Culture in Your Home Stronger than the Culture Deceiving Your Kids* Ventura, CA: Regal, 2008.

Littauer, Florence. *Personality Plus—How to Understand Others by Understanding Yourself.* Grand Rapids, MI: Revell, 1992.

Priolo, Lou. *The Heart of Anger.* Amityville, NY: Calvary Press, 1998.

Smalley, Gary, and Greg Smalley. *The DNA of Parent-Teen Relationships*. Wheaton, IL: Tyndale House, 2005.

Tripp, Ted. *Shepherding a Child's Heart*. Wapwallopen, PA: Shepherd Press, 1995.

Preparing for and Enjoying Adolescence

Arterburn, Stephen, and Fred Stoeker. *Preparing Your Son for Every Man's Battle*. Sisters, OR: WaterBrook Press, 2003.

Campbell, Ross. *How to Really Love Your Teenager*. Wheaton, IL: Victor Books, 1993.

Dobson, James. *Preparing for Adolescence*.Ventura, CA: Regal, 2005.

Ethridge, Shannon. *Preparing Your Daughter for Every Woman's Battle*. Sisters, OR: WaterBrook Press, 2005.

Tripp, Paul David. *Age of Opportunity*. Phillipsburg, NJ: P&R Publishing., 2001.

Understanding the Times We Live In

Comfort, Ray. *Hell's Best Kept Secret*. New Kensington, PA: Whitaker House, 2004.

Daugherty, Sharon. *Avoiding Deception*. Shippensburg, PA: Destiny Image, 2005.

LaHaye, Tim, and Tim Noebel. *Mind Siege*. Nashville: Word, 2000.

McDowell, Josh. *Beyond Belief*. Wheaton, IL: Tyndale, 2002.

—. *The Last Christian Generation.* Holiday, FL: Green Key Books, 2006.

Parsley, Rod. *Culturally Incorrect—How Clashing Worldviews Affect Your Future.* Nashville: Thomas Nelson, 2007.

Understanding Your Teen's World

Arterburn, Stephen, and Fred Stoeker. *Every Young Man's Battle.* Sisters, OR: WaterBrook Press, 2002.

Bradley, Dr. Michael. *Yes, Your Teen Is Crazy.* Gig Harbor, WA: Harbor Press, 2002. Since this book contains quotations of foul language and impure conversations with teens it does not belong on the coffee table at home.

Ethridge, Shannon. *Every Young Woman's Battle.* Sisters, OR: WaterBrook Press, 2004.

Luce, Ron. *Battle Cry for a Generation.* Colorado Springs: Nexgen, 2005.

Ludy, Eric and Leslie. *Teaching True Love to a Sex-at-13 Generation.* Nashville: W Publishing Group, 2005.

Simon, Dr. Mary Manz. *Trend Savvy Parenting.* Carol Stream, IL: Tyndale, 2006.

Understanding the Incredible Potential in Today's Teens

Bevere, John. *The Bait of Satan.* Lake Mary, FL: Charisma House, 1994.

Harris, Alex and Brett. *Do Hard Things*. Sisters, OR: Multnomah, 2008.

Growing Healthy Relationships (or Repairing Damaged Ones!)

Smalley, Gary. *DNA of Relationships*. Wheaton, IL: Tyndale House, 2004.

Understanding Principles of Spiritual Warfare

Anderson, Neil. *The Bondage Breaker*. Eugene, OR: Harvest House, 2000.

Beeson, Ray, and Kathi Mills. *Spiritual Warfare and Our Children—When Your Child Is Under Attack and What to Do About It*. Nashville: Thomas Nelson, 1993.

Gillham, Anabel. *The Confident Woman—Knowing Who You Are in Christ*. Eugene, OR: Harvest House, 1993.

Malone, Dr. Henry and Jack Taylor. Jack *Shadow Boxing*. Lewisville, TX: Vision Life, 1999.

Meyer, Joyce. *The Battle Belongs to the Lord*. Nashville: Faith Words, Warner, 2002.

—. *The Battlefield of the Mind*. New York: Warner Faith, 1995.

Understanding the Concepts of Brokenness and Surrender

Edward, Gene. *A Tale of Three Kings*. Wheaton, IL: Tyndale House, 1992.

Sorge, Bob. *The Fire of Delayed Answers*. Greenwood, MO: Oasis House, 1998.

Growing Your Faith in the Midst of Trials

Daugherty, Dr. Billy Joe. *God Is Not Your Problem*. Shippensburg, PA: Destiny Image 1996.

Smalley, Dr. Gary. *Change Your Heart Change Your Life*. Nashville: Thomas Nelson, 2008.

Building Hope That God Will Deliver

Alcorn, Nancy. *Mercy Moves Mountains*. Tulsa, OK: Harrison House, 2003.

Receiving Emotional Healing

Meyer, Joyce. *The Root of Rejection*. Nashville: FaithWords, Warner, 2002.

—. *Beauty for Ashes*. Tulsa, OK: Harrison House, 1995.

—. *Managing Your Emotions*. Nashville: FaithWords, 2002.

Understanding the Mother's/Woman's Heart

DeMoss, Nancy Leigh. *Lies Women Believe and the Truth That Sets Them Free*. Chicago: Moody, 2001.

Fleming, Jean. *A Mother's Heart*. Colorado Springs: NavPress, 1996.

Understanding God's System of Authority

Bevere, John. *Undercover*. Nashville: Thomas Nelson, 2001.

Nee, Watchman. *Spiritual Authority*. New York: Christian Fellowship Pub., 1972.

Learning How to Pray for Victory in Your Home

Burr, Richard. *Praying Your Prodigal Home*. Camp Hill, PA: Christian Pub, 2003.

Copeland, Germaine. *Prayers That Avail Much*. Tulsa, OK: Harrison House, 2005.

Daugherty, Dr. Billy Joe. *No Fear: Praying the Promises of Protection*. Shippensburg, PA: Destiny Image, 2008.

Gothard, Bill. *The Secret Power of Crying Out*. Sisters, OR: Multnomah Books, 2002.

Grubb, Norman. *Rees Howells: Intercessor*. Philadelphia, PA: CLC Ministries, 1997.

Meyer, Joyce. *The Secret Power of Speaking God's Word*. Nashville: FaithWords, 2004.

Omartian, Stormie. *The Power of a Praying Parent*. Eugene, OR: Harvest House, 2007.

Understanding Today's Body Image Battles

Graham, Michelle. *Wanting to Be Her—Body Image Secrets Victoria Won't Tell You*. Downer's Grove, IL: InterVarsity Press, 2005.

Newman, Dr. Deborah. *Loving Your Body—Embracing Your True Beauty in Christ*. Wheaton, IL: Tyndale House, 2002.

Understanding and Identifying Child Predators

van Dam, PhD, Carla. *Identifying Child Molesters: Preventing Child Sexual Abuse by Recognizing the Patterns of the Offenders*. New York: Haworth Press, 2002.

Healing Sexual Abuse Wounds

Allender, Dr. Dan B. *The Wounded Heart: Hope for Adult Victims of Childhood Sexual Abuse*. Colorado Springs, CO: NavPress, 1995.

Angelica, Jade Christine. *We Are Not Alone—A Guidebook for Helping Professionals and Parents Supporting Adolescent Victims of Sexual Abuse*. New York: Haworth Maltreatment and Trauma Press, 2002.

Brohl, Kathryn, and Joyce Case Potter. *When Your Child Has Been Molested: A Parent's Guide to Healing and Recovery*. San Francisco: Jossey-Bass, 2004.

Kubetin, Cynthia A., and James Mallory, MD. *Beyond the Darkness—Healing for Victims of Sexual Abuse*. Dallas: Rapha Publishing/Word, Inc., 1992.

Morrison, Jan. *A Safe Place—Beyond Sexual Abuse*. Wheaton, IL: Harold Shaw, 1990.

Just for Teens

Etheridge, Shannon. *Every Young Woman's Battle*. Sisters, OR: WaterBrook Press, 2004.

Harris, Joshua. *Sex Is Not the Problem (Lust Is)*. Sisters, OR: Multnomah, 2005.

—. *I Kissed Dating Goodbye*. Sisters, OR: Multnomah, 2003.

Luce, Ron. *Battle Cry for My Generation—The Fight to Save Our Friends*. Colorado Springs, CO: NexGen, 2006.

Ludy, Eric and Leslie. *When God Writes Your Love Story*. Sisters, OR: Loyal Publishing, 1999.

Ludy, Leslie. *Authentic Beauty*. Sisters, OR: Multnomah, 2003.

Understanding Complex Teen Responses

Alcorn, Nancy. *Mercy for...series:*

Cut: Mercy for Self-Harm. Enumclaw, WA: WinePress, 2007.

Starved: Mercy for Eating Disorders. Enumclaw, WA: WinePress, 2007.

Violated: Mercy for Sexual Abuse. Enumclaw, WA: WinePress Publishing, 2008.

Trapped: Mercy for Addictions. Enumclaw, WA: WinePress Publishing, 2008.

2. CONTACT INFORMATION FOR PARENTS

Because of the nature of the fast-paced changes to our children's world, I recommend the following ministries and Web sites as sources for up-to-date news and alerts. Technology and the abuses of technology generally outpace the book publishing pace. So even as these Web sites change, continue to search for new resources.

Helpful Ministries and Web Sites

Focus on the Family, www.focusonthefamily.com; 1-800-A-FAMILY.

Family Life Today, www.familylife.com; 1-800-FL-TODAY (1-800-358-6329).

Joyce Meyer Ministries, www.joycemeyer.org.

Mercy Ministries, www.mercyministries.org.

Teen Mania Ministries, www.teenmania.com; 1-800-299-TEEN.

Institute in Basic Life Principles, www.iblp.org.

ENDNOTES

Chapter 1

[1] Thayer and Smith, *The KJV New Testament Greek Lexicon,* "Greek Lexicon entry for Hodos," available from http://www.biblestudytools.net/Lexicons/Greek/grk.cgi?nu mber=3598&version=kjv, s.v. "ways," Acts 10:13.

Chapter 3

[1] For more information on being filled with the Holy Spirit, visit www.joycemeyer.org and see her book entitled, *Filled with the Spirit.*

Chapter 4

[1] The opening line of chapter 1 in *A Tale of Two Cities* by Charles Dickens, first published in 1859.

[2] John Gill, *The New John Gill Exposition of the Entire Bible,* "Commentary on James 1:17," available from http://www.studylight.org/com/geb/view.cgi?book=jas&cha pter=001&verse=017, s.v. "with whom is no variableness, nor shadow of turning," James 1:17.

[3] Albert Barnes, *Barnes' Notes on the New Testament,* "Commentary on Matthew 6," available from http://www.studylight.org/com/bnn/view.cgi?book=mt&cha pter=006, s.v. "Verse 13," Matthew 6:13.

[4] Ron Luce, *Battle Cry for a Generation: The Fight to Save America's Youth* (Colorado Springs, CO: NexGen, 2005) pp. 81, 97.

[5] Based on information from the Centers for Disease Control and Prevention (CDC), available from http://www.cdc.gov/ nccdphp/ace/prevalence.htm.

[6] Ron Luce, *ReCreate: Building a Culture in Your Home Stronger than the Culture Deceiving Your Kids* (Ventura, CA: Regal, 2008), p. 12.

[7] Thayer and Smith, "Greek Lexicon entry for Skotos," available from http://www.biblestudytools.net/Lexicons/Greek/ grk.cgi?number=4655&version=kjv, s.v. "darkness," Acts 26:18.

8 Based on information from *Strong's Hebrew Lexicon*, available from http://www.eliyah.com/cgi-bin/strongs.cgi?file=hebrew lexicon&isindex=517, s.v. "mother," Genesis 2:24.

9 Based on information from Anabel Gillham, *The Confident Woman: Knowing Who You Are in Christ* (Eugene, OR: Harvest House, 2003).

Chapter 5

1 Based on information from John Gill, "Commentary on Psalm 40:2," available from http://www.studylight.org/com/geb/view.cgi?book=ps&chapter=040&verse=002, s.v. "out of the miry clay," Psalm 40:2.

2 Brown, Driver, Briggs and Gesenius, *The KJV Old Testament Hebrew Lexicon*, "Hebrew Lexicon entry for Bowr," available from http://www.biblestudytools.net/Lexicons/Hebrew/heb.cgi?number=953&version=kjv, s.v. "pit," Psalm 40:2.

3 John Gill, "Commentary on Luke 10:19," available from http://www.studylight.org/com/geb/view.cgi?book=lu&chapter=010&verse=019, s.v. "Behold, I give you power to tread on serpents and scorpions," Luke10:19.

4 George Barna, *Barna Group*, "Most American Christians Do Not Believe that Satan or the Holy Spirit Exist" (April, 2009), available from http://www.barna.org/barna-update/article/12-faithspirituality/260-most-american-christians-do-not-believe-that-satan-or-the-holy-spirit-exis.

5 Josh McDowell and Bob Hostetler, *Beyond Belief to Convictions* (Wheaton, IL: Tyndale House, 2002), pp. 11–12.

6 Barna Research Group, "Barna Survey Examines Changes in Worldview Among Christians Over the Past 13 Years" (March 6, 2009), available from http://barna.org/barna-update/article/21-transformation/252-barna-survey-examines-changes-in-worldview-among-christians-over-the-past-13-years.

7 Ron Luce, *ReCreate*, p. 27.

8 Josh McDowell and David H. Bellis, *The Last Christian Generation* (Holiday, FL: Green Key Books, 2006), p. 13.

9 Thom Rainer, *The Bridger Generation* (Nashville: B & H Publishing Group, 2006), p. 169.

10 Guttmacher Institute, http://www.guttmacher.org/media/presskits/2005/06/28/abortionoverview.html (accessed December, 2009).

Chapter 6

1 John Gill, "Commentary on Psalm 143:7," available from http://www.studylight.org/com/geb/view.cgi?book=ps&chapter=143&verse=007, s.v. "Hear me speedily, O Lord: my spirit faileth," Psalm 143:7.

2 Matthew Henry, *Matthew Henry's Complete Commentary on the Whole Bible*, available from http://www.biblestudytools.com/Commentaries/MatthewHenryComplete/mhc-com.cgi?book=ps&chapter=107, s.v. "Psalm 107:27."

3 A *settled city* can refer to a good place to live; spiritually speaking it represents Jesus, the city of refuge; the church; and ultimately heaven, the city whose builder and maker is God (Heb. 11:10).

4 Prov. 16:18; 1 Sam. 15:23 (NKJV).

Chapter 7

1 American Dictionary of the English Language, 10th Ed. (San Franscisco: Foundation for American Christian Education, 1998). Fascimile of Noah Webster's 1828 edition, permission to reprint by G.&C. Merriam Company, copyright 1967 & 1995 (Renewal) by Rosalie J. Slater, s.v. "OMNIPOTENT."

2 Adam Clarke, *The Adam Clarke Commentary on the Bible*, "Commentary on Genesis 3," available from http://www.studylight.org/com/acc/view.cgi?book=ge&chapter=003, s.v. "Verse 15."

3 Based on information from Adam Clark, "Commentary on Mark 1," available from http://www.studylight.org/com/acc/view.cgi?book=mr&chapter=001, s.v. "Verse 22."

4 Based on information from *Strong's Exhaustive Concordance of the Bible*, available from http://www.eliyah.com/cgi-bin/strongs.cgi?file=greeklexicon&isindex=1849.
Also Thayer and Smith, *The KJV New Testament Greek Lexicon*, "Greek Lexicon entry for Exousia," available from

http://www.biblestudytools.net/Lexicons/Greek/grk.cgi?number=1849&version=kjv.

5 Thayer and Smith, "Greek Lexicon entry for Exousia," available from http://www.biblestudytools.net/Lexicons/Greek/grk.cgi?number=1849&version=kjv.

6 *Merriam-Webster Online Dictionary*, available from http://www.merriam-webster.com/dictionary/dynamite.

7 Based on information from Thayer and Smith, "Greek Lexicon entry for Dunamis," available from http://www.biblestudytools.net/Lexicons/Greek/grk.cgi?number=1411&version=kjv.

8 Rich Mullins, *Never Picture Perfect*, "The Love of God," Geffen Records, 1989.

9 Thayer and Smith, "Greek Lexicon entry for Agapc," available from http://www.biblestudytools.net/Lexicons/Greek/grk.cgi?number=26&version=kjv, s.v. "love," 1 John 4:16.

10 Ibid., 1 Corinthians 13:4.

Chapter 8

1 "The person, blood, and righteousness of Christ, is as a rock, firm and strong, [and] will bear the whole weight that is laid upon it; it is sure and certain, it will never give way; it is immoveable and everlasting; the house built upon it stands safe and sure." John Gill, "Commentary on Matthew 7:24," available from http://www.studylight.org/com/geb/view.cgi?book=mt&chapter=007&verse=024, s.v. "I will liken him to a wise man, which built his house upon a rock."

2 Ibid.

3 Gary Smalley, *Making Love Last Forever* (Dallas: Word Publishing, 1996), pp. 46–47.

4 John Bevere, *The Bait of Satan* (Lake Mary, FL: Charisma House, 2004).

Chapter 9

1 Fictious husband and wife characters in the TV sitcom *Leave It to Beaver*.

² *Merriam-Webster's Online Dictionary*, available from http://www.merriam-webster.com/dictionary/postmodernism%20, s.v. "postmodernism."

³ *Beyond Belief of Conviction*, p. 12.

⁴ Ibid., pp. 12–13.

⁵ Ibid., p.315.

Chapter 10

¹ This doesn't apply to anyone living in an abusive home. Children or adults who are experiencing physical or sexual abuse need to seek help immediately—tell a teacher or a school counselor or pastor, or contact an agency that deals with abuse.

Chapter 11

¹ Based on information from the book by Florence Littauer, *Personality Plus* (Grand Rapids, MI: Fleming H. Revell, 1992).

² Carla van Dam, *Identifying Child Molesters* (New York: Haworth Press, 2002), p. 5.

Chapter 12

¹ For more information on what should be said during a disclosure of abuse, see Cynthia Kubetin and James Mallory, *Beyond the Darkness—Healing for Victims of Sexual Abuse* (Dallas: Rapha Publishing/Word, Inc., 1992), pp. 216, 219.

² My Hope Is Built, words by Edward Mote, music by William B. Bradley; first published in 1836.

³ *Webster's New Collegiate Dictionary* (Springfield, Massachusetts: G & C Merriam Co., 1974), s.v. "condemnation."

⁴ Ibid, s.v. "conviction."

⁵ Gary Smalley, *The DNA of Relationships* (Wheaton, IL: Tyndale House, 2004), p. 83.

Chapter 13

¹ Amy Carmichael quote available from http://www.christianadoption.com/renewingthemind/fame.htm. Original quote taken from a book by Ellen Sanna, *God's Hall of Fame* (Urichsville,OH: Barbour Publishing, 1999), available from

http://www.amazon.com/Gods-Valuebooks-Barbour-Books-Staff/dp/1577484282/ref=sr_1_4?ie=UTF8&s=books&qid=1264029079&sr=1-4.

2 Bruce Wilkerson, *Secrets of the Vine: Breaking Through to Abundance* (Sisters, OR: Multnomah Books, 2006).

3 Norman Grubb, *Rees Howells: Intercessor* (Fort Washington, PA: CLC Ministries, 1997).

4 Dan B. Allender, *The Wounded Heart: Hope for Adult Victims of Childhood Sexual Abuse* (Colorado Springs: Navpress, 2008), pp. 46–49.

5 Joyce Meyer is a well-known Christian author, Bible teacher, and speaker. Her Emotional Healing Kit is available through her ministry or online at http://www.joycemeyer.org/eStore/default.htm.

Chapter 14

1 Michael J. Bradley, *Yes, Your Teen Is Crazy* (Gig Harbor, Washington: Harbor Press, 2006).

2 Joyce Meyer, *The Everyday Life Bible—Amplified Version* (New York: FaithWords, 2006), p. 1585.

3 Billy Joe Daugherty, *No Fear: Praying the Promises of Protection* (Shippensburg, PA: Destiny Image, 2006), p. 19.

Lisa's Postscript

1 *Yes, Your Teen Is Crazy*, p. 11.

2 Paul David Tripp, *Age of Opportunity: A Biblical Guide to Parenting Teens* (Phillipsburg, NJ: P & R Publishing, 1997), p. 19.

3 *Yes, Your Teen Is Crazy*, p. 17.

Tool 2

1 *Identifying Child Molesters*, pp. 3–4.

2 *The Wounded Heart*, p. 52.

3 www.texaspolicecentral.com/childsex.html (accessed April 2009).

4 www.stopitnow.com (accessed 2007).

5 Kathryn Brohl and Joyce Case Potter, *When Your Child Has Been Molested: A Parent's Guide to Healing and Recovery* (San Francisco, CA: Josssey-Bass, 2004), pp. 4–6.

6 *Beyond the Darkness*, pp. 4-5.

[7] Jade Christine Angelica, *We Are Not Alone: A Guidebook for Helping Professionals and Parents Supporting Adolescent Victims of Sexual Abuse* (New York: Haworth Press, 2002), p. 5.

[8] Ibid., p. 28

Tool 3

[1] This information is available from http://www.nlm.nih.gov/medlineplus/ency/article/001518.htm. (accessed April, 2009).

Tool 4

[1] This information is available from http://www.teensuicide.us/articles2.html.

Tool 5

[1] Ray Beeson and Kathy Mills, *Spiritual Warfare and Your Children: When Your Child Is Under Attack and What to Do About It* (Nashville: Thomas Nelson, 1993), p. 3.

Tool 6

[1] This information is available from http://www.troubled-with.com/AbuseandAddiction/A000000968.cfm?topic=abuse%20and%20addiction%3A%20eating%20disorders.

Tool 7

[1] This information is available from http://parentingteens.about.com/cs/drugsofabuse/a/driug_abuse20.htm (accessed April, 2009).

Tool 9

[1] Nancy Alcorn, *Cut: Mercy for Self-Harm* (Enumclaw, WA: WinePress Publishing, 2007), pp. 18–19.

ABOUT THE AUTHOR

Lisa Cherry

Lisa Cherry has seen a lot in 25 years of parenting her 10 children. But the experience of bringing her first daughter through the crisis of being sexually abused by a member of her church was unlike anything she was prepared for.

On the victory side of the pain, she is equipped to share with other parents the essential keys to successfully protecting and navigating children through times of crisis.

Lisa and her husband, Doug, are in their eleventh year of co-pastoring Victory Christian Center of Southern Illinois. Together they also founded REALITY Youth Center in Carbondale, Illinois and Frontline Family Ministries. They have a family radio ministry in which all their children join to discuss multiple facets of developing a healthy, spiritually vibrant family. Lisa has her BS in Nursing from Southern Illinois University.

Lisa and Doug have a passion to see families become united in vision, valiant in battle, yielded in will, and passionate in service for Jesus Christ. Lisa is an anointed Bible teacher who has a special gifting with women, teens, and children. She has been married to Doug for 29 years.

Kalyn Cherry

Kalyn Cherry completed her Bachelors Degree in Social Work at Southern Illinois University in the fall of 2009. She has a passion to see children and youth in this generation avoid the snares of the world, and find the lifesaving power of Jesus Christ. Kalyn is the daughter of Pastors Doug and Lisa Cherry from Carbondale, Illinois. She graduated from Teen Mania Ministries' internship program, The Honor Academy, in 2005. Currently, Kalyn is employed by Victory Christian Center and REALITY Youth Ministry in Carbondale. She is also working for Southern Illinois Regional Social Services Crisis Counseling Team.

Kalyn loves both the challenge and the fun of living a life on the edge in the everyday realms of ministry, family, and work. She is engaged to be married to Adam Waller in August of 2010.

WE INVITE YOU TO JOIN:

Frontline Families Ministries

A Coalition of Families:

United in Vision... Yielded in Will... Valiant in Battle... & Passionate in Service to our Lord Jesus Christ!

go to: frontlinefamilies.org

Micah, Tara, Nathan, Lucas, Kalyn, Matthew, Hannah, Lydia, Josiah, Lilibeth, Rebekah, Ethan, (Clockwise from Left), Doug & Lisa

- Listen or Purchase Radio Shows aired on various stations
- Speaking Engagements
- Family Day Conferences
- DVD Teachings
- Books

Doug & Lisa pastor Victory Christian Center of Southern Illinois
Post Office Box 460, Carbondale, IL 62903
(800) 213-9899